The Smoke over Xanadu

Corinda Pitts Marsh

ISBN: 9798397444040

DEDICATION

This story is dedicated to the brave and good people of Ukraine. May they have peace and destroy their invaders, for in our world today, the evil are many and the good are few.

CONTENTS

Kubla Khan · i

1 All Should Cry, Beware, Beware! · 1

2 A Sunny Pleasure Dome · Pg 14

3 A Damsel with a Dulcimer · Pg 21

4 Caverns Measureless to Man · Pg 27

5 Many an Incense Bearing Tree · Pg 41

6 That Deep Romantic Chasm · Pg 65

7 Beneath a Waning Moon · Pg 87

8 Close your Eyes with Holy Dread · Pg 116

9 A Savage Place · Pg 134

10 The Milk of Paradise · Pg 156

KUBLA KHAN

BY
SAMUEL TAYLOR COLERIDGE

In Xanadu did Kubla Khan
A stately pleasure-dome decree:
Where Alph, the sacred river, ran
Through caverns measureless to man
Down to a sunless sea.
So twice five miles of fertile ground
With walls and towers were girdled round/
And there were gardens bright with sinuous rills,
Where blossomed many an incense-bearing tree;
And here were forests ancient as the hills,
Enfolding sunny spots of greenery.

But oh! That deep romantic chasm which slanted
Down the green hill athwart a cedarn cover!
A savage place! As holy and enchanted
As e'er beneath a waning moon was haunted
By woman wailing for her demon-lover! And from this
chasm, with ceaseless turmoil seething,
As if this earth in fast thick pants were breathing,
A mighty fountain momently was forced:
Amid whose swift half-intermitted burst
Huge fragments vaulted like rebounding air,
Or chaffy grain beneath the thresher's flail;
And mid these dancing rocks at once and ever
It flung up momently the sacred river.
Five miles meandering with a mazy motion
Through wood and dale the sacred river ran,
Then reached the caverns measureless to man,
And sank in tumult to a lifeless ocean;

And 'mid this tumult Kubla heard from far
Ancestral voices prophesying war!
The shadow of the dome of pleasure
'Floated midway on the waves;
Where was heard the mingled measure
From the fountain and the caves.
It was a miracle of rare device,

A sunny pleasure-dome with caves of ice!
A damsel with a dulcimer
In a vision once I saw:
It was an Abysinnian maid
And on her dulcimer she played,
Singing of Mount Abora.
Could I revive within me
Her symphony and song,
To such a deep delight 'twould win me,
That with music loud and long,
I would build that dome in air,
That sunny dome! Those caves of ice!
And all who heard should see them there,
And all should cry, Beware! Beware!
His flashing eyes, his floating hair!
Weave a circle round him thrice,
And close your eyes with holy dread
For he on honey-dew hath fed,
And drunk the milk of Paradise.

1
2030: ALL SHOULD CRY, BEWARE, BEWARE!

In 2020 many were plagued by disease, poverty, and fear, but that all began to change a few years later. Disease was being wiped out by Artificial Intelligence, a power stronger than mankind could have ever envisioned—stronger than its creator. Poverty abated when Loki stepped in to aid those less fortunate. The fortunate were finally forced to pay their fair share, and fear began to abate when all were guaranteed a high school diploma without the usual trials and trauma. College became a given for any who desired a title added to their name. Difficult classes disappeared from the curriculum in of all but a few chosen schools. No longer were youthful minds burdened by the likes of calculus and bio-chemistry: we had AI for all that, freeing us to pursue more pleasant pastimes. No longer would we be required to study the likes of Coleridge and Shakespeare. Life began to be a joy for all with no requirement to labor with reflective thinking or endless investigations to find truth. Later came the final star on our crowns. We no longer had to dread old age, for now the benevolent Loki would transport us to a Utopian Paradise, Paradise Valley, our own personal Xanadu. They even provided luxury transportation to this idyllic spot of ground—the train to Paradise.

Samuel Taylor Coleridge described it perfectly in 1797, long before we actually realized it could exist. He envisioned a ruler named Kubla Khan as the creator. Ours was a man called Loki in the newly formed zone called Ragnarock.

In Xanadu did Kubla Khan
A stately pleasure-dome decree

And so it was Paradise Valley came to be. Some, however, resisted this direction, preferring instead to struggle with life and keep what measure of independence man can own. Independence, unfortunately, comes with a heavy price. A few unnamed souls saw doom instead of Xanadu in this generous offer. And even fewer were bold enough to challenge the direction of government late in

2029 when they could see the train approaching rapidly toward the zone. Two of these men were Miko Maheegan and Bjorn Olafsson, a scientist and his protégé.

Loki alone recognized the threat these men posed and sought to eliminate them before they could bring down his ultimate plan. Late in 2029, we find Bjorn and Miko fleeing as the Paradise Express makes its trial run to the Paradise Hotel, where fortunate senior citizens would soon be able to live in total luxury for the duration of their lives, making way for others to conduct business without the burden of caring for the elderly. Healthcare was about to become another of the many privileges Loki would provide in the benevolent spirit of Xanadu.

Bjorn was 47 years old and Miko was 65 when the danger became so obvious that both of them were willing to risk their lives to save civilization. They were among the few who still clung to learning and thinking as their lifeblood. Loki was unaware of Bjorn's involvement in Miko's plan, but he recognized the threat Miko posed, so he gave orders to find him and bring him to headquarters for re-training. Miko was to be brought in regardless of the circumstances of his capture: as long as he was brought to Loki, his condition was irrelevant. Loki and his men were unaware that Miko had created an exact doppelganger who shadowed him at all times.

When Loki's Select Nine closed in on Miko, Miko shouted to Bjorn. "Run, Bjorn, run!" Bjorn knew what those words meant, and he knew what to do. The Alpha Wolf was about to be loosed. Their task now was to disappear, unnoticed like vapor in the night. They were so close, close enough to smell Paradise Valley. Even they didn't know how close, but they still had not found it.

Miko Maheegan would always be the Alpha Wolf. He was cunning and vicious with his enemy. He knew the ways of primeval man—the ways that led to survival, but he also was schooled in the methods of modern science. He was lethal to an enemy, always using both modes of survival—modern and primeval. What the dark side feared most was his brain. The State would destroy him—if they could. They knew they would never control him or his brain. They knew what would happen if they didn't.

Sooner or later Miko would find the answers he was looking for. The minions sent to destroy him had no idea why they were chasing him. They simply followed orders with steadfast dedication mixed with a hefty dose of fear. They had seen what happened to others who lacked zeal when carrying out orders. They were told to destroy Miko Maheegan. They were told he was the number one enemy of the state. They had an electronic signature, and they detected it dead ahead. The State had provided them with an image and they saw that image running beside the tracks. The esig matched the image, or at least it was close.

Miko Maheegan was an enigma to all except one man. He was not easy to know even when he was young. There was always something different about him. As a child he had spent hours alone or at the heels of an ancient Algonquin Shaman who was as strange as he. He spoke little, but anyone could see wisdom in his eyes. He had ancient memories that guided him and shielded him from harm. He was always shadowed by a large gray wolf.

The old man who was his closest companion died when Miko was seven years old, but Miko continued to go to the creek bank where the old man had breathed his last breath. Miko shared his blood line through an ancient link. Sometimes the wind spoke to the boy, and he replied with a language others could not understand. Even his grandfather left the child alone when he went to the creek. None of them knew about the cave where the old Shaman lived. But Miko had known about it before he was born on the farm beyond the cave. The wolf lived there and hunted along the creek beside the boy and the old man. The boy knew no fear. He understood the wolf, the old man, and the eagle, but not other children.

The boy grew into a man, a large and

physically powerful man, but he was no less enigmatic than he had been as a child. He excelled in his studies and entered the university when he was 15, having gone beyond the material available to him in traditional school. When he was 24, he graduated with doctoral degrees in both engineering and physics, but his knowledge exceeded either field. He was a lone wolf among sheep. Only one woman dared to breech his boundaries, and she couldn't stay.

Bjorn was not too different from Miko, but he was younger and only slightly more civilized. He came to the university not many years after Miko began teaching, back in the day when studies were rigorous, and only the few earned the golden tassel. Since Bjorn had declared physics as his major, he was assigned Professor Maheegan as his advisor. He was a top student as Maheegan had been, but he still managed a more normal persona even if it was a disguise.

Bjorn was tall and lean with thick blond hair, a gift from his Norwegian heritage. His skin was fair but flawless, and his chiseled profile made him attractive. He, however, shunned social interaction in favor of deeper studies. More than one female vied for his attention, but he escaped all serious relationships. Instead, he spent his time with his mentor who became his closest friend. The attachment between student and professor was instant. Professor Maheegan saw in young Bjorn a promise of significant scholarship, but it was the other potential that bonded the two.

Bjorn obviously sensed the direction the State was taking. Both men knew the danger men face when they surrender control of their destiny to evil. Neither man was intimidated by the risk of his convictions. Miko had been Bjorn's friend and mentor since the first day he walked into Maheegan's office in the fall of 2005 at the university. The two men, however, hid their friendship for reasons both understood but neither spoke about. A cloak of silence and distance had served them well. Only Yona came close to bridging the space between them, but even she was not aware of how close she was and what her role would eventually become.

Bjorn respected no one on Earth more than this giant of a man, but the dark side feared him above all men and possibly above all forces, natural or otherwise. He was a threat to their control, and a tyrant treasures control—ultimate control. A mind that cannot be controlled is always to be feared. It was October, 2029, and life for all was about to change.

When Bjorn heard Miko shout, he ducked his head and sprinted toward the cover of the glade. The tree cover would not protect him, but it would provide cover until he could reach the hidden passageway. The men in black fired one shot in his direction as he ran. Blood ran freely from his cheek. The bullet only grazed his fair skin, but still blood ran thick and hot. He never lost a step. His long legs carried him with unusual speed. Adrenalin pumped through his veins, and determination doubled his speed. Too much depended on his survival, but the survival of his mentor could determine the fate of the human race. The world did not know Miko Maheegan, but if they were successful, his name would go down in history. If they were not, the world, or at least their part of the world would cease to exist.

Bjorn peered one final time from the cover of the trees at the unfolding scene before he vanished. Miko's self-created doppelganger chased his creator toward the train. The two images appeared identical, but one had a slightly different gait, more mechanical. The images seemed at times to merge into one.

Nine men in black state uniforms chased the two images, thinking them to be one. Miko ran to gain enough distance to cross in front of the silent advance of the train. The menacing train sped toward its destination on forced air as the world appeared to move in slow motion. Miko barely made it across the tracks ahead of the engine, but his doppelganger was severed by the bullet-sharp nose of the train as it gained speed. The doppelganger's head rolled, bloodless, off one side of the train channel while the electric impulses and blasts of air supporting the speeding train mangled the still writhing body crafted in total duplication of its creator.

The nine state officers halted by the train looked on with supreme pleasure as the cars advanced almost silently toward their destination. They had gotten their man. Passengers on the train peered from the windows at the nine as if they did not see them. They continued to gaze out the windows as the train picked up speed and disappeared from view.

When the last car cleared the body, the nine advanced as one to examine their kill as hyenas descending on a carcass. The glade 100 meters to the south remained still and silent except for the screech of a large eagle flying south. Mangled bits of something resembling bloodless flesh and a few scattered primitive chips lay on the tracks in front of them. Those remains were not as they had expected.

"The slippery bastard got away! We can't let this get out. The son of a bitch got us again!" shouted the leader of the group.

"No, we got him! I saw the train hit him! We got him!" another shouted. He was young, still green and cocky. He was a handsome fellow but not the smartest in the group, but then most of them were not exactly on the cutting edge of the scientific realm. They were followers, true believers of Russian descent, raven haired and empty headed. They would lay down their lives for the cause—for the greater good—just as they and their forefathers before them had been taught. They were sworn to serve the Commissar and would be rewarded accordingly. They would always have their needs met and would never be burdened by thoughts and decisions. They trusted their leader without hesitation. They were lemmings near a cliff they could not see.

"You fool! Look what we got, nothing but a doppleganger!" the captain answered. The nine advanced as one toward the tracks. Loose shreds of bloodless skin waved in the wind. Other unrecognizable parts rolled slowly around inside the confines of the slim titanium channel. The head had come to a stop against a small rock six meters away. Instead of blood running from the remains, only sensors were visible inside a mostly empty polyethylene skull. "Gather this shit up! Just bring the head. I've got a plan."

The men picked up the remains of Miko's doppelganger and loaded them into the PKU van. All of them accepted the logo on the side of the van without question. The People's Kleptocratic Union kept the meaning of that logo and many other facts to themselves. It worked to their benefit not to tell the minions more than was necessary.

The nine men scrambled into the van, shoving the debris aside as they sat. The youngest of them got in the driver's seat. He tapped the console to program their path. The captain, sitting next to him, whispered. "No, not that way." The captain reached over and reprogrammed the route. The young cadet wrinkled his brow and stared at his superior but did not attempt to correct the route. He had been successfully programmed to do as he was told. Past experience kept him from resisting.

Still, the cadet whispered, "But that's…"

The captain glared at him with hard black eyes. The cadet turned his face to the road again and avoided further eye contact with his superior. Five minutes later the van came to a smooth halt in front of another less pleasant and slightly sparse clump of trees where tattered tents were stretched loosely over a group of community outcasts. These "undesirables" were not allowed into Ragnarock, but government vehicles regularly delivered supplies and "medication" to them.

Five very thin men in their late 20's or early 30's wandered around mumbling to no one in particular. They looked up only briefly as the van approached. The captain motioned to one of the senior men in the group. He nodded toward one of the staggering men who was rather larger than the others. "That one," he said. Then the lone man stepped out through the rear door of the van. He knew what would happen next.

The man approached the group without any sign of emotion. He selected his target and plucked him from the group. The others walked on like zombies seeming not to notice the departure of their comrade. The man who had been singled out was tall and more muscular than the rest, approximately the same height as weight as Miko Maheegan and with the same tanned leather skin pigment. The man in black leaned the stranger against the van then turned him to his side with his back facing the stand of trees. He stuck a gun to the complacent man's chest. The man didn't appear to notice. He did not move but did exactly as he was told. A hollow point bullet passed silently through the man's heart and exploded against his spine. The man dropped to his knees and collapsed, lifeless, on the ground.

The captain motioned to two of the officers in black. They jumped out of the van, carrying the empty head of the doppelganger. They knelt beside the body and stretched and pulled at the polyethylene head until it fit snugly over the dead man's head like a Halloween mask. Blood flowed freely from the man's chest. The officers waited until the blood ceased to flow then pulled out a metallic woven blanket and rolled the body into it until he appeared to be a chrysalis in a cocoon.

They loaded the body into the van, laying it across the foot space for the rear seats. The men got in and propped their boots on the body. The van drove away without a sound, leaving no trace of its presence. The men in the encampment continued to walk around mumbling inaudibly.

2
A SUNNY PLEASURE-DOME WITH CAVES OF ICE

The next day the Commissar's official channel announced with great sorrow that one of Ragrarock's most revered scientists, Miko Maheegan, had been fatally injured by a speeding train and would be buried in a celebrated state funeral. The Commissar expressed his condolences to the family and offered his apologies for not being able to have a public viewing since the body was so tragically mutilated by the accident. Only the family viewed the body and their visit was quite brief.

The Commissar made a grand speech about the event saying, "Fellow citizens, this is one of the most compelling reasons to have everyone scanned so that they can be protected by the Doppler Halo. Had we known that this eminent citizen and valued scientist was in the path of the train, perhaps we could have prevented his demise. We could have halted the train before it reached him. That is the reason for our urgent protocol for implanting our citizenry with this new discovery. Unfortunately Dr. Maheegan, had not been chipped and scanned. We deeply regret this tragedy. It is a supreme loss to our scientific community and our Ragnarock populace. Don't let this happen to someone in your family.

With DH, we can keep you and your loved ones safe. No longer will any children or hikers be lost. We will always know how to find them. No longer will any of you need to carry identification for any reason because we will automatically know who you are and where you are at all times. And most importantly, there will be no crime since we will know precisely where everyone is at all times. A geosynchronous satellite run by the state will provide this security for us every second of every day. We can virtually eliminate the need for police and for guns as there will be no crime.

This system will protect human life just as we have protected your finances by eliminating physical currency. Thanks to our forward thinking scientific community and conscientious government officials, you are no longer burdened by having to carry cash or the long-outdated personal checks. Please assist us in this important endeavor. Each baby born in Ragnarock is being chipped and scanned at birth, and each citizen will likewise be chipped and scanned at mobile units set up around the city for your convenience. From now on when you go into a restaurant, you will not be required to present ID, and the robots will even know your usual order so you can be served more efficiently and promptly. Ragnarock will be the best of all worlds as we embrace a very promising and secure future, unlike our neighbors who have chosen not to join us.

Paradise Valley will be completed next year so that each and every one of you will have the opportunity to retire to complete luxury at age 65. It is such a shame that Dr. Maheegan did not survive so that he could have lived in happiness in retirement. He suffered the tragic accident when he still had a few more years of brilliance to share with the rest of us.

My deepest sympathy goes out to his family. Dr. Maheegan did not have children of his own, but he was fortunate to have a niece and a nephew as well as a brother and sister-in-law who will miss him terribly. It is a tragic day, indeed, for Ragnarock. Let us all offer our condolences to Dr. Maheegan's family."

A grand state funeral was held with the family in attendance. They paid homage to the body of a homeless man in an elaborately carved mahogany coffin buried in the Ragnarock City

Cemetery with Mr. and Mrs. Adriel Maheegan and their children, Yona and Quinn in attendance. They had been a very close family, particularly Yona and her Uncle Miko. Yona was 45 at the time. She was teaching at the same university where her uncle had taught before he left his post five years earlier. He had been doing private research since that time, which was a thorn in the side of Ragnarock's reigning elites.

After the funeral, Yona tried to talk to her parents about her uncle's death, but they could not or would not answer her questions. They went to the mobile unit set up near their home and had their implants done the following week. Quinn was much younger than Yona and was ill, so they told Yona it was best for Quinn if they all cooperated with the government. Yona, however, knew that her Uncle Miko would never have consented to be chipped. He had resisted all efforts to control him all his life, as had she. She, however, finally relented for the sake of her brother.

Quinn was denied treatment until Yona was implanted with the chip. She made her appointment six weeks after her uncle's death. It was an ordinary day, on an ordinary street, in an ordinary building— except that nothing about it was ordinary. She drove to the location and parked in a long row of spaces reserved for others set to receive the chip. Most of them were like she—they had resisted for one reason or another. She had her own reasons. Her uncle had told her just enough for her to be highly suspicious of Ragnarock's current government. At this point, she trusted no one, but if she refused, her brother would die. She had no choice.

Yona sat in her car more than 30 minutes before she took a very deep breath and got out. She had a dark, foreboding feeling. Perhaps it was her spirit bear warning her, but she had no choice. She hated the thought of the government's knowing where she was and who she was. Three women walked ahead of her toward the building. She could hear bits of their conversation. They were much younger than she.

"Julie, I think this is great! I don't feel safe to walk alone at night, but now I will be protected."

"I don't know, Julie. Something about this scares me."

"Oh Nancy, don't be ridiculous. It won't hurt at all. They will numb your skin first. You are such a sissy!"

"Julie, do you have any idea how this could bite us in the ass?"

Caroline intervened, "Girls, stop picking at each other. It will be fine. Just trust the Commissar. What could go wrong?"

Nancy relaxed a bit and answered, "I suppose you are right. We really don't have a choice, do we? They are withholding our pay until we get it done. Ok, here we go."

They reached the door and Nancy pulled it open. The smell of alcohol floated out the door. Yona always hated that smell. She had since the day they first took Quinn to the hospital and the doctors gave them the news. Quinn had ALS. Yona had enough education to know what that meant. That was one of the medial problems doctors had not been able to conquer. He would die from this malady. Maybe not soon, but he would die. He would not live into old age. Caroline was the last of the three women to enter, so she held the door open for Yona and smiled at her as she walked in.

Yona nodded but did not speak. She took another deep breath and walked forward to the waiting area. She swiped her device as she walked through the door and waited to be called. Nancy was called first. She smiled at Yona and the other two women as she got up and walked to the waiting attendant. Yona felt nauseous and sweat popped up on her forehead. She had to do this. She knew that, but every fiber in her body told her it was wrong. When she was called, she turned her shoulder to the attendant and received the implant squarely between her shoulder blades. It was carefully placed to ensure that she would not be able to touch it. She was warned against that.

Quinn was immediately granted special treatment for his ALS, but he did not improve. They waited for medicine as a child waits for Christmas when he knows the family cannot afford presents and Santa is dead. The following year Paradise Valley was completed and the government started trying to assure the Maheegan family that doctors in Paradise Valley were better equipped to handle critical cases like Quinn's.

3

A DAMSEL WITH A DULCIMER

When Paradise Valley was completed, a special train took a select group to tour the facility. On board the train were Loki's journalists and photographers. They recorded the visit in full…or so Loki said. They were lulled to sleep by a Damsel with a Dulcimer playing mesmerizing music piped into each train car along with the heavenly scent of pine forests and cooling streams.

The train sped along the tracks while the passengers enjoyed a gourmet meal and beverage. Passengers chatted contentedly, so much so that they became unaware of their surroundings for a portion of the journey. They stared out the windows without seeing the landscape. None however seemed aware of their exact location. They were enraptured by the beauty, almost as it if it were not real.

After what seemed like just a brief moment in time, they pulled into an elaborate station, designed as a replica of Grand Central Station in New York City. The giddy passengers were duly impressed. They stepped from the station directly into an equally grand dining room. The room was encircled by superbly painted walls with replicas of ancient Roman sculptures and paintings by the old masters. One recognized a Rembrandt instantly. Another pointed out a Degas and a Renoir. All were amazed at the beauty surrounding them. When they looked out the windows a lush green landscape surrounded the building with paths leading into the most gorgeous park any of them had ever seen. One large mansion was situated just south of the main dining room, just far enough away for privacy.

The passengers wandered about and found their tables, as hand crafted place cards marked each of their places at the table. When all were seated and quiet, Loki stepped up to the podium and adjusted the microphone. "Welcome to Paradise," he began. "What you see here is the future in store for each and every one of you when you reach the grand age of 65. No more will you need to wonder if you will be able to afford to live comfortably in retirement. The state is now going to guarantee you a life of luxury and leisure for the rest of your days, and if you should become ill, you will be afforded the very best of healthcare at absolutely no cost. The lovely building to your left will house the best physicians and medical equipment available to man today. Even if younger people become ill, they will be afforded the same care as they will be brought here for treatment. They can come here to convalesce and be treated by the country's finest doctors with the latest drugs and accommodations.

Now, please, each of you enjoy your dinner and the entertainment so you can return to Ragnarock and tell your friends and family what a magnificent facility they can look forward to when their day arrives. Unfortunately we must close the gates of Paradise Valley when we leave, and we cannot allow visitors, but we have the latest technology to keep future residents in constant contact with their loved ones so you will not miss them at all.

Every detail has been considered and accommodated for your permanent peace and happiness. This is just the first of many buildings that will be constructed. A tour of the grounds will be conducted after dinner, but I'm afraid it will be limited for your safety. We are still in the process of securing the area, so for the present, fences have been erected to keep you safe. Rest assured those unsightly fences will be replaced with acres of gardens and cottages for all who will come here in the future."

The diners were in awe of their surroundings and murmured to each other quietly as they ate, while occasionally pointing to a piece of art or a spray of lovely flowers in a marble vase. Even the ceilings in the room were painted so that the fire preventive nozzles in the ceilings were disguised as flowers dotted about the structure. Loki ensured them that the room had all the latest safety features, and if there were ever a fire in the building, those lovely "flowers" would quickly douse the blaze and save all their lives. The sheep were amazed by the insight with which the lions had constructed the grand hall.

When dinner and the tours were concluded, the sheep filed back onto the trains to Ragnarock while small robots collected the dishes and swept the room clean. The dazzled citizens happily headed home. All were pleasantly tired and slept most of the way as a result of a tasty glass of wine and the most peaceful music, which was once again piped into each car.

When the train arrived back in Ragnarock, the passengers were met with ever more curious friends and relatives. Each departing passenger was aglow with reports of the most magnificent retirement facility they could ever hope for. All the electronic billboards around town flashed photos constantly of the new facility at Paradise Valley. Eager citizens gazed at the glossy images and chatted about how much they looked forward to retirement now that Loki had provided so well for them. Their hefty taxes would certainly be worth it.

No one questioned how much it would cost or where the money would come from. They had long since left those things in the hands of their trusted government, a government that would take care of them from cradle to grave as long as they followed the rules, and most did. Sheep always do. Yona, however, preferred to question and follow her own rules. Fortunately, she had learned very young to keep her thoughts to herself and to keep her head down, out of the line of sight of hungry lions.

In late August of the following year, Yona held her pale and critically ill brother's hand for the last time. She kissed his cheek just before he got on the train headed for Paradise Valley. She knew intuitively she would never see him again. She looked ahead and saw dark smoke hovering over the trees in the distance. Her mother cried and her father tried to be strong. Yona was neither strong nor emotional. She knew too much.

She drove home alone and went to the basement. She turned up the sound of ocean waves to fill the room. She took from the shelves her worn and dog-eared copy of Nietzsche's *Thus Spake Zarathustra*. She sat in the blue chair in the corner reading until she finally fell asleep. Her father woke her late into the night and told her to go to bed. He was quiet and kind with his words. He knew what she was feeling. She was attempting to deal with something she could not change, and she understood too well, just as he did.

4
CAVERNS MEASURELESS TO MAN

In the year 2030, civilization changed. Not all at once, but bit by bit the changes came as man accepted the protection offered by the Doppler Halo. Freedom was etched away by man's intense desire for safety and guaranteed protection—his desire for a father. Predators and prey became separated into distinct yet invisible classes. Human genomes determine at birth which we will become, but before the halo, prey instinctively hid themselves from the predators. Prey used weapons to defend themselves and stealth to avoid danger. But with the DH, they would no longer be able to hide, nor would they need to. They were told by the lions that predators would no longer exist.

Sheep turned their protection over to the mighty lions. Hungry lions dressed themselves as shepherds, and the sheep perceived them as such. But there were wolves among them who could not be tamed. They are the third species of mankind. Miko Maheegan was such a man. Wolves are dangerous animals—they protect only their own pack. They dwell in dens, away from the sheep and the lions. Lions are unable to reach the depths of the wolves because wolves are thinkers and allies of the eagles. They thrive alone devising their own protection aided by sharp-eyed eagles.

Nietzsche's Zarathustra sought the silence and isolation of a cave to contemplate life, but such contemplation is unsettling and usually unsafe. Since man stood upright, he has seen the cave as a place of safety and protection, but the thinking man is never safe and knows he must protect himself. Weaklings fear him most of all. It is only his mind that protects him. Those who wish to rule over him will never allow him to be safe. He will be safe only when he brings the hammer down the final time.

Zarathustra walked with the eagle at his back. One lone man walked with a large gray wolf at his side and an eagle flying over his head outside the official realm of Ragnarock. He lived in a cave by a river bank, undetected by the lions and undeterred by the sheep, but this had not always been so. He was to be feared by the lions most of all. He was the unseen guardian of the Sheep. He was part wolf and part man in their midst unnoticed.

His shelter was a stone crack in the earth called Maheegan's Cave. On his shoulders rested the fate of mankind.

Man himself threatens his kind. When left unchecked, he becomes the lion. The Doppler Halo gave the lions the perfect weapon with which to control the sheep. The lions rounded up the sheep and kept them in the confines of their realm and promised them protection. Only the wolves refused and withdrew to their dens, caves in the hills. They would neither be identified nor ruled, but they were few and the lions were many. The lone wolf with the eagle over his head was their only hope. Miko Maheegan was this man.

DH was a flawless system. It always worked. Everyone would be safe. The scans began in 2030, some refused. Most were hunted down and convinced to comply. A few escaped. One was Miko Maheegan. His brother complied but for his own reason. Maheegan's ancestors were native to a harsh land and survived the white man's onslaught. They held to their land and slowly adapted to the new ways, but some kept the old ways deep inside. Miko was one of those. He wore the look of the new for disguise, but his soul bore the mark of another world where men were free and brutality was a necessity for survival. His ancestors feared nothing and had no use for white man's currency. A man who has no fear and doesn't love money cannot be controlled.

Maheegan was a wolf. He was destined to bring down DH and restore humanity to his world. The lions believed they had eliminated him. His niece never believed the story as it was told by the Commissar. She, too, was a wolf, but she had been scanned in 2030 for reasons beyond her control. She lived under the thumb of the lions, but never completely under their control. Her cellar was her cave. She was a thinker. She was unaware that her Uncle Miko was still watching over her and was trying to save her from her apparently inevitable fate. But had she known that fact, she would not have been surprised. Somehow she still sensed his presence in her life.

The lions had devised a system through which each citizen was provided a perfect life at age 65 in a retirement community where every desire was satisfied. Utopia, Paradise, Xanadu, everything for everyone. Transportation was provided for each sheep on his, her, or its 65th birthday, which would arrive for Miko's niece in 2050. Time was closing in for Miko. He would give his life to save hers. As time closed in on Yona Maheegan, she began to keep a diary, writing down the thoughts that troubled her in the night. Her diary recorded her thoughts, most of which her uncle could read as they passed through her brain.

Miko was 85 years old in January of 2050.

His companion was a massive almost black wolf named Tom, and before Tom a gray wolf of the same pack, both with keen yellow eyes and a will to protect their human. A large mature eagle nested in the ancient oak tree leaning over the creek bank. The wolf brought his prey to the mouth of the cave and gave his man the choice parts and the eagle the remnants after man and beast had eaten their fill. Both were lean and strong even as they aged. The wolf lived between the two: man and bird of prey. The three lived in harmony, each filling a role. The eagle watched, the wolf protected, and Miko plotted and devised. Their aim was to save Yona and as much of her world as possible. The plan had been slowly developing over the 20 years the trio had lived in the cave.

Twenty years earlier, Miko had disappeared into a hidden copse as his doppelganger was decapitated by the train. A secret search party scanned the countryside for weeks after that fateful day, but they never found any trace of the man they feared most. They suspected his capability, but they were powerless to control him. He had primitive battle skills handed down through countless generations, and he had the will to use them. These were skills unknown to AI because they were born of something beyond logic. Primitive warriors used strengths innate in the will to survive, strengths that overcome the science and technology of modern man. Modern man has lost his edge as he sharpens his knowledge of the artificial.

A few modern geniuses got close to Maheegan during those years, but they paid the ultimate price for doing so. One was a clever lieutenant who ventured too close to Maheegan's Cave on a winter's day before the weather was tamed.

The eagle screeched and the wolf made a low menacing sound. He crouched near the entrance of the cave and showed his sharp, white teeth. Miko pointed toward the far corner of the sacred cavity in the earth, and the wolf crouched as he moved in that direction. Miko waited beside the entrance. The hapless intruder stepped inside and gasped when he heard the ancient sound of a warrior. Even he recognized the sound of death. He screamed only once before his throat was slit. His scalp bled profusely as it was hurled into the sky. The eagle caught it in mid-air. Wings flapped as the eagle took his next meal and landed in the nest above. The wolf crouched and waited for his portion. The rest was thrown to the alligator in the meandering creek below the cave.

The chip implanted in the shoulder of the young man in black was removed and reprogrammed so that he appeared to be scaling a mountain on the opposite side of the world. Fellow officers never figured out how he got to Nepal in such a short time or why he was attempting to climb the mountain in the dead of winter. His corpse was never found.

Miko smiled when the job was done. Tom was young then and sat proudly at his side. He laid his hand on Tom's head and stared into the forest rimming the creek bed. The large cold blooded reptile slapped the cold creek water with his tail as he slid into the darkness of his own cavity in the creek bank.

Miko remembered the day he "died." Bjorn was with him that day. Bjorn was fair skinned and unlike Miko, but only in appearance. He also had the heart of a wolf and courage of a warrior. He had descended from another warrior cult long ago, a cult of fair-skinned, ruthless men in the land of fire and ice.

On the day of Miko's official death, Bjorn stood beside him and watched the van disappear over the hill after the men in black realized they would not find Maheegan or his companion. They feared he was still alive, but he had vanished into the mist along with his accomplice. When the van was out of sight, Miko and his protégé emerged from the opposite side of the copse and began the trek to the cave.

They had ten miles of relatively benign terrain to cover and both were fit, so they reached the cave before midnight. Bjorn's small wound had ceased to bleed, but he went to the creek and washed the blood away then rubbed Miko's herbs into the gash.

Miko knew the ways of the Shaman as well as the ways of the university. Both men were intimately familiar with the cave. Miko had played there as a small child and had been preparing for this time since those days. His grandfather had warned him of this day decades earlier. When Miko heard him chanting unrecognizable sounds, he asked his grandfather what the sounds meant. The old man just patted his head and told him, "You will know when your time comes." Young Miko looked at the old man's brown and wrinkled face and believed him. He never asked the question again. But when his time came, he knew.

In 2050 Maheegan's Cave had most of the comforts of a modern home. Five generations of Maheegans had used this lair. It now had electricity and a bank of computers to continue his work. The machines linked themselves to an eye in the sky. But on the day Miko "died," it was still relatively primitive except for the few pieces of electronics that Miko had been gathering for this day, which he knew would come. Miko and Bjorn sorted out some of their immediate problems on the trek to the cave. Others would take time and cunning.

Miko was well aware of the workings of the DH and was very close to a solution to the problem.

Bjorn avoided detection using Miko's device, but for their plan to save his family, they needed more time. Miko had gathered materials to make a diamond shield to jam the DH signal. One prototype was on the rock ledge just inside the cave. But he needed time to carry out his ultimate plan. Neither realized it would be twenty years before their ultimate plan would be executed. They were not even sure what their ultimate plan would be.

The two men entered the cave silently. Miko opened a bottle of wine resting in the hollow rock in the wall where the spring rose and overflowed. The water flowed down the edge of the cave living area in a smooth trough hollowed out by constantly running water. It made a pleasant sound as it splashed into the creek below after leaving the mouth of the cave. Miko uncorked the wine made from the fruit of the vines hanging over the cave entrance. He poured it into two stone cups. Both men drank before they spoke.

Finally Bjorn said, "Well, Miko, I suppose you are officially a dead man by now." He smiled at his mentor.

"Probably so, but they know that is not a fact, so they will keep looking. You need to reappear at home very soon or they will suspect things we do not want them to suspect."

"Yes, I will go when day breaks. It will take me two days to get back home, but I can explain it away if anyone asks. I'll say I cut my face while working in my garden. They blow hard, but they are a bunch of dumbasses, so I'll make them believe. They have no idea how much time I have spent with you."

"Bjorn, do you know Yona?"

"I've seen her at the university, but I don't think she would know me. I only know her because of you, and she would not associate us. Why do you ask?"

"She only lives one block away from you, and I need you to watch over her. They are going to come after my brother sooner or later. He's her father. Her younger brother is ill, and I fear they will take him when they get Paradise Valley up and running. That will be very soon."

"Miko, what is Paradise Valley...really?"

"You don't want to know. I'm not certain, but I have a pretty good idea. I have several colleagues who have given me clues. I think they will all go into hiding, and I will try to communicate with them. We must find a way to defeat the system, or we will all die. Paradise is no paradise. I can assure you of that. I think they will open it in the next month or so. I think I know where it is, so I will try to get close enough to find out what happens there. Nothing good will come of it, and you don't want to go. Keep working at your lab, and make sure they believe you are valuable to them. That is the only way to survive long term. You will have to become a skilled actor. Try to contact my brother and assure him that I am safe. Tell him to keep his head down and remain unnoticed. I will try to get messages to him, but it may take me some time before I can do that. It is important that he not question my disappearance or my death."

"Do you think they will come after him?"

"I don't know. If they question my death, they most likely will. Yona's brother, Quinn, is very ill. He has ALS, so they need to do what they have to do to take care of him. Yona is very close to him, but she's definitely got a mind of her own, so she's the one I'm most worried about. Sometimes I can read her thoughts, so I know how much danger she could be in.

I will train you to teleport your thoughts to me so we can communicate. It is a skill I learned long ago from an old Shaman who used to go hunting with my grandfather. They were blood brothers and descended from the same ancient ancestor. He lived near this cave and was like an extra grandfather to me. He was alone, like I've always been. His only friends besides my family were animals. There is a wolf pack living in the hills to the north, and he could sit in the middle of that pack, and the wolves would come to him as if he were their chief.

The Shaman's name was Little Feather. He taught me much. He knew of this cave. I think he had come here with my grandfather years earlier just as I had. He helped me to make it more habitable. He hewed the trough for the spring water during the last years he lived. He told me it would someday be life-giving. He believed in a mystical presence that hovers near us at all times. He was not religious, but I would call him spiritual. When I was young, I followed him everywhere. He taught me to identify animal tracks, to grow corn, and to kill deer and cure the meat to survive the winter. He had hunted with my grandfather's people. He taught me other skills that I will not name.

I can live here outside society because of Little Feather and my grandfather. I think he is still here in the cave with me. Sometimes I can hear him speaking. Strangely, it is his voice and not my grandfather's that I hear most often."

Bjorn left that day and made his way back into Ragnarock without notice, but his life was never the same again. Over time, Miko taught him to read Yona's thoughts. Miko crept into Ragnarock under the cloak of night occasionally and Bjorn returned to the cave many times. Both men lived in a solitary existence keeping to themselves only, while continuing to work toward a common goal.

Soon after Miko's "death," Bjorn followed Miko's sister-in-law several blocks and watched her as she turned into her driveway. He parked two blocks away and got out of his car and started jogging down the sidewalk that ran along the street in front of her house. As he reached her house, he called out, "Hello, Ma'am. Can I help you with that package?" At the same time, he folded his arms in such a way as to flash a pre-arranged ancient sign from Miko.

Della Maheegan was stunned and stopped for a moment. Bjorn made the sign once more. Finally she smiled and said, "Why yes, this package is quite heavy. Thank you."

Bjorn trotted up to her and took the heavy box she was lifting from the rear of her car. "Miko is alive and well," he whispered just loud enough for her to hear. Then he said much louder, "Where can I put this for you, Mrs. Maheegan?"

"Right here will be fine. Thank you very much. I am so glad you came along." She smiled at him, but the tilt of her head told him she still was a bit wary of him.

Bjorn slid a prewritten note into the fold of the box and said, "My pleasure, Ma'am. Have a nice day." And he trotted off in the direction of his car.

The note explained what Miko wanted his family to know but warned them not to search for him. He told them he was at their old family homestead but they must not come there. Few ventured out into the countryside by that time anyway. It would bring suspicion on them all if they were to try to contact him. Although the weather had turned warm, there was a fire that night in the Maheegan fireplace and tiny white ashes floated into the night.

Della scanned the streets for this unnamed man each time she went out from that day forward. She would see him occasionally, but most days he would merely nod and acknowledge her presence. Only twice after that was he able to deliver a message. The last one was 24 hours before the accident. After that, he settled into an unnoticed existence in his house in the next block, but he continued to surveil the Maheegan home on Elm Street. He would keep Yona safe as long as he could, but she failed to notice his presence. Her life was a jumble of emotions and struggles that filled her consciousness and blinded her to his presence.

5

MANY AN INCENSE BEARING TREE

Yona questioned many things. She was unaware that Bjorn had been watching over her for many years. Her diary recorded her thoughts, but even she did not know why she was writing them down each day. She began recording her thoughts after Quinn went away, but it was in 2050 as she approached her 65th birthday that she became more assiduous about keeping a record each day. Those thoughts could get her into more trouble than she knew how to handle, but she no longer cared. Bjorn did care, however, and so did Miko. Both listened to her thoughts as she wrote them. Both feared for her life, but she did not, at least at first. As August grew closer, however, she began to sense the smell of death in the air around her.

January 23, 2050

Dear Diary,

Main Street in Ragnarock, Alabama, is dotted with small cafes where contented residents sip aromatic tea from delicate china cups while sitting at quaint Victorian tables placed in orderly fashion on pleasant sidewalks. The sidewalks are lined with colorful crepe myrtles. Neatly enameled wrought iron benches are placed conveniently along the boulevard. The diners are all healthy, beautiful, and dressed in similarly perfect attire: Perfect individuals in a perfect world. The weather, having been regulated by dedicated scientists decades earlier, is nearly always perfect.

If not for the presence of certain devices, passersby might believe the year to be 1950, not 2050, and the season to be late spring instead of the rawest days of winter. Everyone is completely contented. Contentment, however, is often confused with complacency, or should that be complacency is mistaken for contentment? Either way, I have my questions, which I can only ask here, Dear Diary. Hear me out and you decide. To write is to know—thus I write.

Robots guided by small, almost invisible surveillance cameras keep the benches dusted and the sidewalks immaculate. A scrap of paper or a crumb of food landing on the sidewalk is instantly scooped up by miniature, stainless steel robotic elephants with vacuum cleaner trunks. Their vision is as sharp as the jungle animals they resemble. They miss nothing and record everything in their photographic memories. The robotic civil servants stuff debris into a pouch in their belly. The contents of these metallic janitors are emptied into a communal incinerator at the end of each day after having been examined by selected servants of the Commissar. I suspect that records are kept of certain offenders.

Most of this goes unnoticed by oblivious diners. Peace and tranquility dominate the cheerful populace of Ragnarock. They move about with the same secure precision as their robotic servants. If not for the occasional foreboding clouds of smoke appearing above the artistically chiseled horizon, this would be the perfect town in the perfect time. It is the result of the Zone's experiment in creating a utopian society, an endeavor attempted repeatedly throughout history, but never before successfully. Loki determined that he would be successful. He took over a large area of the state through some rather shifty means and reshaped it for "his people."

I don't know how all this came about, but something about it makes me ill, not that I would ever dare to say so. That's how it works: we don't say anything and we get everything. That smells to me.

Even writing these private thoughts makes me nervous, but I feel compelled to do so—why I don't know—yet. My fear is that someday I will find the answer. I shall hide these thoughts each day in the small crevice in the north corner of the stone fireplace my grandfather built with his own hands— for as long as I can keep my fireplace. Grandpa hauled the stones from his father's creek bank and placed them one by one, leaving the crevice and one loose stone for secrets. I wonder if he knew I would need to keep my secrets safe one day in the future. Maybe he was Orwellian. I've been looking for answers since Quin went away, but so far all I have is questions.

I was 45 when Quinn became ill. He was only 20, and until he became ill, I didn't realize how much I loved him. My parents adopted him after I began working at the university. His parents had abandoned him, so my family stepped up to provide him safety and love. When he went away, I quickly discovered how much I loved him.

Quinn was a smart boy, but the best part of him was his heart. He seemed to understand life far beyond his years. He had ALS, and that was back in the late 20's, so we didn't have the advanced care we have today. The Commissar made arrangements for him to go to the hospital at Paradise Valley in late 2030.

We never saw him again. His doctors

communicated with my parents. Finally they told us they could not save him. He passed away in Paradise Valley without his family at his side. They told us he was doing much better then suddenly, they said he was gone. Even they could not save everyone.

I wanted to see him before he passed away, but they said it was too late. He was already gone. I'm not sure anyone realized I had been messaging him late at night and sometimes he answered. His answers seemed cryptic and didn't seem like him at all, but they made me wonder. Once I asked him about his cat. I asked him what I should feed the cat. His answer talked about how much he loved the cat and wanted me to take good care of him. He said I should give him salmon. He said the cat loves salmon. Quinn never had a cat. He hated cats. They made him sneeze.

I tried to blow that off as maybe he was on medication that affected his memory, but later I began to figure out a few things. After mom and dad died in that awful car crash and Uncle Miko was gone, I was alone. I was fearless. Not much mattered to me in the first year after I lost my family. As time went on, I realized no one ever comes back from Paradise Valley.

Mom and Dad never wanted me to ask too many questions. Unfortunately, questions are what I'm all about. Mom and Dad seemed nervous. They had been that way since Uncle Miko died. Every time I asked about Uncle Miko, they hushed me up. It was as if they were hiding some big family secret. Hiding something from me always makes me curious. I think that is the reason I wanted to teach literature. I like delving into a mystery, but this mystery was one I was cautioned against time after time. I don't like being told I can't do something. I never have. That's probably the trait that separates me from my dear friend Lillian.

Poor, sweet Lillian obeys the rules, always. Unfortunately, however, she doesn't keep secrets well, so I don't tell her the contents of my little round of skull. They would scare her to death, and she would tell everyone she saw. She has been my dearest friend for more than 50 years. Today she wants to meet me for lunch. We are both rapidly approaching the ripe old age of 65. We all know the significance of that magic time, but we are most certainly not all equally excited about its implications.

Lillian is giddy about her imminent departure from Ragnarock, but then Lillian is giddy about lots of things. She sees it as an "eminent" departure—not me! I know it is only looming—definitely not a thing of great worth. She has no problem with believing in the immanence of the much lauded Commissar, which is something I fail to see. Funny how three words that sound the same can have such vastly different meaning. Etymology is another interest of mine that completely annoys Lillian. Etymology, entomology, it's all the same to her. Words bug her. Bugs bug me, oh well.

Lillian is fair-haired and kindly, not like me at all. My flaming red hair presupposes my temperament even now as it is shot through with silver shards. I got my hair from my sweet Irish mother, but most of me is true to my Native American father, who was fearless and intelligent. He treasured his heritage as did my Uncle Miko. I trust no one and tend to be recalcitrant and hard-nosed, unlike my gentle life-long friend. I'm not what you would call hot tempered, but I do enjoy a little verbal skirmish now and again. Not Lillian—she has heart—I have backbone. Together we make a perfect team, more or less.

Sometimes I wonder who I'm leaving these words for and why. I have no children, no one to leave them to. I guess it's for my grandfather who built the fireplace. Maybe he's still hanging around somewhere to read them. I like to wonder about things. That might be the reason I like Nietzsche. His cave seems like a place I'd like to reside, at least for a while.

Thinking and talking to animals holds far more allure to me than talking to people. Come to think of it, the only two-legged creatures I like are birds. I like four-legged critters, not six, not eight, not two—only four. They are the ones you can trust. I really don't even trust Lillian, and we've known each other almost all our lives.

Lillian and I will soon face a drastic life change not anticipated by residents of Ragnarock in the past, but welcomed by Ragnarockians in 2050, or at least most of them. Ragnarockians of the past had what government officials tell us was a flawed system called Social Security to rely on when they retired, but the fortunate citizens of 2050 are promised something far better than that antiquated system.

Just like me, every piece of furniture in my house is a holdover from the past. That's just the way I see things. I see life through the wrong end of the telescope.

I, too, am a holdover from the past, not unlike my Uncle Miko, who perished in a battle with a freight train, or so we were told. Even that, I question, in the privacy of my hold-over brain. I was teaching at the university when Uncle Miko died. I knew even then that the story we were fed did not ring true. My mother cautioned me never to talk about my doubts with anyone, not even family. Both of my parents died not many years after that, but I never heard them speak again about Uncle Miko.

The only time I made a serious attempt to talk to them about Uncle Miko was a few days before they died. My father simply looked at the ceiling and put two fingers of a shaking hand to his lips and shook his head from side to side. He was cautioning me—then he was gone. He and my mother both died in a horrific car crash as they were on their way to their favorite café to celebrate their anniversary.

Uncle Miko was the joy of my existence when I was a child. He was 20 years older than I. He was a real-life hero to me. He could talk to the wildest of creatures, walk right up to them. His voice seemed to hypnotize them as it did me. He was brilliant and larger than life, both physically and in my own myths. He stayed on the farm with my grandparents most of his life and still maintained his workshop right up to the night he died.

Uncle Miko had a workshop behind my grandparents' home with fascinating tools I could never identify. He could build something from nothing. He was a master of mechanical gadgets. He was an anachronism and was larger than life. He clung to our Native American heritage more tightly than the rest of the family. The most fascinating part of his workshop, however, was in the basement where he kept magical electronic equipment.

Miko was my father's youngest brother and didn't seem so old to me, so we were closer than most uncles and nieces. He tolerated my presence when I was a little kid. He didn't seem to mind if I watched him work. Even before he graduated from college, he was always tinkering with electronics and making what I thought was magic. Even though he earned a doctorate in physics, he was never successful in his professional life at the university. He was not a team player. He always marched to a drummer no one else could hear. A few of his students did hear his drum, however, and they clung to his every word. When I was older, I met some of them, and they told me how much they learned from him. They all insisted he was a true genius.

His entire workshop burned the night before the accident. That night my father told me he was chasing those responsible for the fire when he met his demise. My father never talked about that incident again. By the time my grandparents died, just two years after Uncle Miko, most people lived in the city, so the farm was abandoned and the forest on the land became wild again.

Farms were no longer necessary since city factories began producing all the food needed for daily subsistence. The food produced in the factories looked exactly like the food I had eaten as a child, but somehow it never tasted quite as good to me. No one ever replaced Uncle Miko or the farm in my life.

Now no one ventures into the countryside. We are all city dwellers, like it or not. Big Brother

Loki watches over us here in the city. George Orwell was way ahead of his time. We are told we are safer here and that the forests and fields are dangerous places we should avoid at all costs. I knew a different world, but I can never talk about it outside my dark basement walls. I know better, but sweet Lillian grew up believing what she was told. She didn't have an Uncle Miko.

When Lil and I were born in 1985, civil unrest was common in Ragnarock, just as in other cities, but fortunately, that is no longer the case. People in Ragnarock have changed as well. Most adapted slowly and sometimes painfully to the new way of living, but life goes smoothly for us now, unlike earlier residents of the turbulent past when the press stirred up constant problems for the citizenry.

Back then every country boy (and some of us girls) was armed to the teeth and didn't hesitate to defend his life and property, which of course, led to chaos. Now we are a more obedient citizenry. We have no problems. At least that's the official line, which Lil has swallowed hook, line, and sinker.

Flocks of sheep, we are today. Perhaps I am only disguised in sheep's clothing. Disguise is important in these idyllic days. It usually is. Something that looks too good to be true usually is. Rarely do we receive something for nothing, but those who do the receiving usually close their eyes and open their hands.

Ragnarock is now guided by the illustrious Commissar Loki. When Loki took control, he promised the populace a form of Paradise none had ever imagined (and I didn't choose to imagine his world—I had my own version of perfection). We are all obliged to celebrate his guidance. All is well in Ragnarock as reported in the *Ragna Daily News*, the official news source of our enviable community. Our Chief of Disinformation keeps us clear on what is true and right.

Each of Ragnarock's fortunate citizens has been guaranteed a reservation in Paradise Valley, the ultimate luxury resort. No longer do citizens have to work long after retirement age. Now each and every one of them is able to retire in luxury at Paradise Valley Resort at no charge whatsoever. In Paradise Valley every need and even the slightest desire of its residents is immediately satisfied.

The problem lies herein: This coveted end requires total obedience. Unfortunately I have never been known to be particularly docile and rarely obedient. The fact that I have escaped notice so far truly amazes me and scares the crap out of Lillian. If she knew half the truth about me, it would scare her to death--literally.

Lillian has always seen the good side of everything, so she anticipates her 65th birthday as a five-year-old would Christmas morning. Never known as a deep-thinker, she is, nevertheless, kind and optimistic. She has always done what she was told and has difficulty understanding why I am so recalcitrant. The fact that I don't want to retire to Paradise Valley is a complete mystery to her. More tomorrow, Dear Diary.

January 24, 2050,

    Dear Diary,

    I arrived at the bistro ahead of Lillian and chose a table next to the wildly blooming hibiscus shrub. The yellow blossoms fit the color scheme of the bistro. The very congruity of my surroundings nettled me. Too much contrivance. I prefer the rocky edge of a mountain stream, but we are no longer allowed that option. Loki tells us we have all we need right here within the walls of Ragnarock. Anything we don't have, we can call up on our large screen walls, and there we are! Perfect life, so perfect, he installed walls to keep non-citizens out. He says we can't have others coming in to steal what we work so hard to maintain.

    Lillian's delicately freckled face wrinkled with glee as she approached me. She was all giggles and wiggles as she took a seat beside me. Even her walk irritated me today—too prissy, just too damned happy! "Hi, Lil! I see you are in fine fiddle today."

    "Why shouldn't I be? I'm almost there, you

know."

"Yes, you are. I suppose we should raise a glass to that thought."

"We should!"

As if by magic the robotic waiter rolled up to us and said, "Ladies, what would you like with your bubbly. Some celebratory Greek salads with tomatoes perhaps—with a splash of vinaigrette, I believe it is? And maybe some Key Lime pie to finish?"

Lil giggled once more and said, "Isn't it amazing how he knows exactly what we want? I wonder if he read my mind."

"Lil, he heard what I said about celebrating, and he knows your face. What do you usually order when we come here? If he's up to reading minds now, I'm pretty sure I should hesitate to drink the Kool-Aid he brings me."

Slightly insulted, Lil replied, "Why a Greek salad? He could have offered a Caesar salad. But still I think the technology is amazing."

"You would," I mumbled.

"What's that, dear?"

"Nothing," I replied.

I stared blankly off into the smoke above the trees. Unfortunately though, my recalcitrance did not leave her speechless.

Lil resumed her elated musings on her near future. "Oh, Yona, I hear Paradise Valley is divine!

Simply divine! We've worked all these years and paid into the system. Now we finally get to reap the rewards. I can't wait. I'll turn 65 on the 15th of March, and the magic train will be waiting."

Lillian sat up quite straight in her quaint perfectly sculpted, wrought iron chair and smiled broadly as she spoke. She jostled the remaining lettuce on her plate, looking for the final bits of ripe tomato. One of the wee elephants swept by her foot, snatching up the thin magenta-rimmed slice of radish that had fallen from her plate. She shifted her foot slightly to accommodate the little creature without realizing it. Lillian failed to notice. She accepted his presence like she accepted everything else.

Lillian always smiled that same inane smile. Sometimes I wanted to take a Brillo pad and scrub it off her face. I saw the humor in remembering those old scouring pads people used before all homes were cleaned by robots. I smiled in spite of myself for longing for those days to return. Even I saw the irony in my wanting to return to scrubbing floors and sinks with Brillo pads. I must have lost the rest of my marbles.

Lillian's crystal blue eyes twinkled as she continued to babble without interruption, "Of course, they don't call it a train, but you know I still live back in the olden days. What is it they call them now? My memory slips now and then. I guess that's why they want us all to catch the bus at 65, metaphorically speaking, of course. I definitely have slipped downhill since I hit that magic 60 mark." She giggled that ridiculous giggle again. Its effect on me was akin to being goosed with an old-time cattle prod. I winced and rolled my eyes.

I resented that last remark. The over-obvious eye roll gave me away as I watched faceless souls ambling down the bustling street. "I don't know about that Lillian, I like my job. I'll miss working with the students. And besides, I think that should be my decision like it was in my grandfather's time. He continued to work his farm even after he had a stroke when he was 85 years old. That's the way he wanted it! When he could no longer walk, he crawled down the rows digging potatoes. He liked feeling useful. And they call that atrocious thing they send for us *The People's Magic Carpet*. If you ask me the old bus line was much better. There is nothing magic about that monster with all its frills and menace. And for the record, my memory is just fine!"

In Lillian's opinion, sometimes my memory is a little too good. She frequently wishes I would forget certain moments in our past—like the crush she had on Ralph, the bus driver, when we were in the 9th grade. I couldn't resist, "Lil, I bet you remember Ralph! Now that was a real bus driver!"

There it was, the giggle again before she

replied with a childish red blush, "Yona! How dare you! I was only 14."

"See, your memory is just fine! And you must agree he was a lot better than the robots we have today."

"Well, yes, he was better, but the robots do a great job of driving the bus and the trains drive themselves. I think that's great. You know I met Fred riding that old bus. Fred was the best friend I ever had. It seemed logical for us to marry later, but I don't think I knew how much I loved him until he got on the train to Paradise Valley that day." A sudden and rare look of melancholy crept over the incessant grin on her face like a summer cloud.

I almost felt bad for bringing up Fred's name. I knew she was never really passionate about Fred, and he was a good guy. I would have been grateful to find such a man to marry, but somehow, that option escaped me. Maybe I never married because I have too many questions and no answers. I have searched all my life for answers, but none seem to be forthcoming.

I smiled at Lil, but my eyes searched the streets without knowing what I was looking for. It seems I've always searched for something out of my reach. I've always wanted answers to unasked questions. Or maybe I've been simply trying to escape. I don't even have an answer for that.

The elephant moved toward my foot, but I

refused to give ground. He bumped my foot rather harder than anticipated, but still my foot was planted in place. He left a scrape on the side of my leg. The tiny monster had to back up and go around me. I glared at him and muttered, "Little shit! Go away!" A tiny trickle of blood crept over my ankle and into my shoe.

These little bastards were accustomed to total obedience and obedience has never been my long suit. I made a mental note of the tiny red flash the elephant shot at me when I called him a little shit. I probably should not have done that at this particular time.

"Yona, he's just doing his job! Be nice!" Lillian said, still wearing that inane grin. She didn't notice my unease, but then she rarely does. She argued, "Yona, you must remember we need to make way for the younger generation to take over. They must have jobs to take care of their families. We must step aside for the greater good. You know what they say, the greatest good for the greatest number…it is our time to do our duty to our community, and besides, I think it will be a world of fun. No more Monday mornings at the office for me! I say hooray for us. Let's ride the Magic Carpet. I, personally, have never liked setting an alarm clock and going to work to do a job I think is useless. I don't feel needed like you do. I just feel used. I'm ready to catch the bus or ride the magic carpet or whatever it is they call it. It will certainly be a fairy tale adventure for me!"

I told her, "Yes, but what if that fairy tale is 'Little Red Riding Hood and the Big Bad Wolf'? I just don't trust Loki. Retirement might be right for you, Lillian, but I know I'll miss working. I don't think I'm ready to drink their Kool-Aid. I like getting up in the morning and looking forward to seeing the faces of my students. Some of my students have become like my kids, the kids I never had. And on top of that, I don't qualify for another six months. I'll miss you terribly!" I suddenly became aware of the blood oozing into my shoe from the wound left by the persistent elephant, but I was not about to acknowledge the injury.

Lillian shouted at me in an angry whisper, "Yona! Keep your voice down! You don't want anyone to hear you say anything bad about Commissar Loki. You know he's very sensitive about his reputation. He has worked tirelessly to create the perfect society for us. He will think you aren't a team player, and you don't want to lose your spot in Paradise Valley. Besides, you know they have the computers all set up for us to communicate. I'll message you every day and tell you what great fun we are having."

An expression of tenderness came over her face and she continued in a less angry whisper, "Fred will be there. The Commissar was very kind to give him an early dispensation when he was injured several years ago. That's how accommodating they are. Commissar Loki is very compassionate about things like that. Fred's job injury was causing him so much pain, the Commissar gave him an early arrival ticket. Fred says life over there is fantastic. His leg doesn't even hurt anymore. And he looks great. I hardly recognize him when we chat. He even sounds different. I guess it is the super equipment they have over there in Paradise Valley. They have the best doctors in the world there, and everything, I mean absolutely *everything*, is free. There, even being old is fun! The people I know don't even seem to age once they get there.

All you have to do is put in an order to get anything you want. I just know I'm going to love it. I have been told I'll be housed with Fred, next to Al and June. I can't wait! One thing that does puzzle me though is where exactly is Paradise Valley? They tell us they can't disclose the actual location because there would be riots with people trying to get in early. I'm sure they keep it secret for our personal safety. They can't have everyone there. Some of us have to stay here and work."

Lil shielded her lips with the side of her hand and whispered, "Did you know they have a separate place for Congress and the Commissar?" Lil didn't seem to notice, but the mechanical elephant with his eyes and ears alert edged closer to Lillian. He was attempting to park himself directly under her chair. I blocked the persistent elephant so he could not hear everything Lillian was saying. Next he tried to attack my other ankle, but I kicked the little shit out of the way.

I cringed as Lillian prattled on. "I only found out when my son was a congressman for a few years. He opted out, but he would never talk about it. I accidentally saw a memorandum tucked in his jacket pocket when I took some of his clothes to the laundry. He doesn't know I know. It would get him in huge trouble if he disclosed that. They call their place Nirvana to distinguish it from our ordinary Paradise Valley. I bet they have much nicer accommodations than we do. On the other hand, people in Paradise Valley say they want for nothing at all, so you can't beat that." Lillian was totally unaware of the grimace on my face or the robotic surveillance.

The wind shifted and I could smell the faint odor of smoke. I became aware of the ominous but faint gray plumes over the tree line on the horizon without realizing it. My eyes surely had glazed over as I considered what Lillian was saying. Lillian obviously has already drunk the Kool-Aid. The Nirvana comment struck a nerve, but I kept my surprise to myself. Lillian needed to stay in her fairytale world, so my thoughts were best secluded in my little round of skull as usual.

If Nirvana were on the up and up, why should it be a secret, and why would Congress members need a separate place for themselves if Paradise Valley were actually Paradise? Still, how would the chosen few get to Nirvana since everyone leaves on the same train? Or do they? Sometimes the Commissar sends two trains. Why? I had never noticed who was getting on which train, but I certainly would in the future.

None of the Paradise Valley residents seemed to be aware of this fact. I had never heard of anyone mentioning it to those they left behind. Something was surely amiss, but then I had always harbored doubts about anything Loki had to say. His speeches rang with the chimes of deceit every time he opened his mouth. Instantly, answers began to form in my mind.

A long pregnant pause ensued, making Lillian nervous. She wrinkled her brows and leaned forward as she looked at me. I'm sure she saw the wheels turning but she never seemed to guess where they were going. This time, it was best she didn't know my thoughts.

I sat up and re-directed the conversation, "Lillian, do you know what they call a group of quail?"

"Why no, should I?" Lillian answered. Her expression changed in a flash from concerned to puzzled. She stared into my face and paused her fork in midair.

"A Covey, that's what they are called, and a group of pelicans is called a flock." I'm sure my previously friendly tone held a thinly veiled note of mockery. A fly landed on the rim of my glass. I blew him away and pushed the glass to the side, no longer pretending to share Lillian's celebratory mood.

Lillian was visibly annoyed and had no idea what I meant. "Yona, what on earth do you mean? Why would I care about bird congregations?"

I shifted in my chair as the elephant came for me again. I was ready for him this time, but I wished for some of those old pointed-toed spike heels women used to wear before a more comfortable mode came into fashion. "Well, what do you think a group of baboons might be called?"

Lillian became totally annoyed. She had no idea where I was going with this, but she was sure she didn't want to hear it. "Ok, I give up. What is a group of baboons called? I guess this is part of your teaching process. Go ahead and educate me." Sarcasm was not her forte.

"A Congress, that's what they call a group of baboons, a congress of baboons!" I forced my gaze past Lillian focusing on the street again. She twisted her lips to the side as she considered that fact. The citizens are fools destined to become prey for the baboons, but sweet Lillian would never acknowledge that fact because she was prey by nature.

"Yona, I think it is time for me to go! I'm not going to let you take away the fun of my journey. Maybe you need to see Doctor Emanuel. I think you need medication!" Lillian folded her napkin neatly and laid it beside her plate then got up and walked away.

I didn't bother to answer. It wouldn't do any good anyway. Lillian walked briskly toward her car but looked back as she rounded the corner in front of the bakery. The smell of hot scones mixed with the faintest hint of smoke settling on the street. The sun was creeping behind the neat row of buildings. A chill suddenly settled over me. Still I could see the smoke in the distance.

6

THAT DEEP ROMANTIC CHASM

Dear Diary, I sat at the table sipping iced tea until the obnoxious elephant approached again. Suddenly I tossed my napkin in his path and got up and started slowly walking down the sidewalk, thinking all the while about Lillian. I had always loved Lillian and in some ways admired her innocence, but sometimes I wanted to smack some reality into her. Then it occurred to me that a dose of reality might be a much too bitter pill to swallow, at least for Lillian.

Let Lillian live in her fantasy world where life is perfect. Reality is rarely perfect, but it will always be real. Even when truth is bitter, we must swallow it if we are to endure. One possible and even probable reality smacked me at that moment: None of us would survive the truth of this existence.

I still don't have the answers, but now I see some of the questions more clearly. Nirvana and Paradise Valley are certainly very different entities with very different populations and realities.

Living in a fantasy world without thinking, while it can be exquisitely intoxicating, is often quite dangerous. Lillian has been a bit "light under the hat" since we were kids. Occasionally she has wagged her happy tongue in inappropriate venues and caused calamities for others.

Once, she casually mentioned the contrary opinions of her friend, Daphne, to her office manager. Daphne had simply questioned something one of the town's senate members had said about local taxes. Daphne was never seen again. Reality bit them both, but Lillian never connected the dots.

I never called her hand on it. She would not have believed me anyway. The dots began to connect themselves as I walked past idyllic shops with brightly colored decorations where oblivious customers were smothered in smiles and crippled by convenience.

I have learned what to say and what not to say even in my classroom. Some ideas are simply no longer tolerated. When I began teaching, I could pull local and national news articles from various news sources for topics to discuss in research and writing classes, but that ended in 2030 when Loki took over the media, promising citizens the same coverage for a much lower price. First they attempted to control our opinions by instituting a Disinformation Officer, who weeded out any incorrect information for us, but that wasn't effective, so the government came up with a better solution. Officials insisted that having several different reporters covering the same event was a waste of money, so they hired the very best writers and reporters for the official network. The rest were given more useful jobs.

It made perfect sense to most people. It went against everything I believed in as a professional educator. I was relegated from that day forward to towing the party line instead of educating students to find truth, no matter how well veiled. When information is shackled and only provided by those who wish to control the masses, everyone suffers one way or another, including those who hold the handcuffs.

Resistance to this shift was deemed unpatriotic and punishable. I learned how to side step, but I had to control every word that came out of my mouth or across my screen, and I became very conscious of the company I kept. The hardest part of this scenario is living a lie every minute of the day. The daily battle inside my head is destroying me. I tell myself I can endure and fight, but the fighter is becoming punch drunk. I think this is what boxing enthusiasts call a TKO. They haven't completely knocked me out, but they have almost done me in.

Fortunately, my basement is still filled with boxes and file cabinets containing articles collected during years of teaching. I also maintain a personal library to rival most community libraries of the past. Of course libraries no longer exist in Ragnarock. They have all been replaced by computer banks that can access "true" material.

One of my particularly treasured articles was written in 2009 by a bioethicist who started the current trend in health care with his Reaper Curve. The Reaper Curve dictated that only the useful members of society got medical treatment. The very young and the very old were deemed useless, so they were left to die rather than use precious resources to save them. It was expense not worth the dollar. His ideas led directly to the establishment of Paradise Valley Resort. I strongly suspect, at this point, that the Reaper Curve is controlled by a "Grim Reaper."

These resources are from that transitional era when the first hints of a societal shift began. I own a copy of Bradbury's banned novel, *Fahrenheit 451*, and the even more ancient, *Time Machine* by H.G. Wells, and George Orwell's *Animal Farm*. I guard these printed treasures with my life. They are now banned material. I am fully aware of what would happen if anyone found them.

My home is ancient and quite modest, but it has a secret basement where this library exists. I am happiest when I sit in the midst of these treasures, basking in the scent of old books—a smell like no other. I have no idea what to do with all these materials when I am forced to ride the Magic Carpet, but now I see that it will come for me just as it will come for Lillian—but far too soon to suit me. I've considered setting explosives to destroy the entire building after I've made my final exit. Maybe that's what Uncle Miko did. Maybe it was he who set the fire. Maybe he knew they were coming for him that night.

This brought pleasant memories of Uncle Miko's basement. It was much like mine except it hid gadgets and machines instead of books. I would never want a stranger to live in my home and find my library. What might they do to the library when they discovered it, which sooner or later they would? I'd rather see it go up in a blaze I had set rather than to see it in the hands of the wrong person. My students should have these treasures, but that would surely endanger their lives, so it might be best to destroy them when I go. I have no heirs and no one to trust my legacy to without putting them in jeopardy.

Suddenly the impact of these facts crushed me. I sat down on one of the wrought iron benches. The intricately woven black iron felt cold against my back, sending a chill from my neck to my toes. My chest felt tight and my eyes widened. I sat in utter stillness until my heart rate slowed and I regained some measure of composure. If only there had been birds singing in the tree beside the bench, if only. I remembered the sound of birds and slowed my heart. Birds and the rushing stream behind my grandparents' farmhouse—those are the sounds that still my heart.

I closed my eyes and remembered another day with pear trees in bloom. White blossoms with pink centers, petals falling to the earth. Hurston's story of a girl with a "pear tree" love. Shelling peas on a warm front porch. Rocking chairs creaking as they rocked. Catching catfish in the stream. Bathing in the cold creek on a summer day. Climbing trees to look into a bird's nest. Flying kites on a windy day. My cousin Sam. The smell of my grandmother's kitchen in the early morning. Hot biscuits with a hole poked in the middle to pour syrup into. All gone without a protest, not even a whimper. Traded for a perfect world that ended with a train ride to Paradise Valley.

I still live in the same house I was born in even as most others have taken nicer apartments provided by the government. My house is small and rather modest, but the basement makes it special. As far as I know, no one, including Lillian, is aware of the basement except the few carefully chosen students I have brought to my inner sanctum. The secret room serves, not only as a private library, but also as a convenient storage area and as a private place for me to meet with Nicoli, Anya, and Christian.

The current law requires that the house become common property of Ragnarock on the fateful day I leave for Paradise Valley. That date will be the Ides of March for me, not literally, of course, but figuratively.

For Lillian it is a literal fact, but she has yet to connect the dots. I'm pretty certain she has never read Julius Caesar anyway, not that she would associate that with her own Ides of March.

Home owners are no longer allowed to sell their homes, but my ownership was grandfathered in when my parents died. It cannot, however, be sold or transferred to anyone else when I leave since only one generation can inherit. It will become common property for Commissar Loki to distribute or use as he sees fit. It will be used for the infamous "common good," a phrase I abhor. When the "common good" rules, life is commonly unpleasant for all or at least for all the common people.

When I continued walking toward my house, I suddenly glimpsed what I perceived to be a familiar figure, or at least someone I thought looked familiar. I was one block from my house when an elderly man who looked very much like Uncle Miko slipped between two houses where a gate had been left open.

I quickened my pace and called out, "Uncle Miko!" as I followed after him. I ran into the back yard through the open gate calling after him, but he disappeared. A dense hedge of vines and small trees completely obscured the bamboo fence around the property, so I thought he might be hiding there.

I was looking around for him when the man who lived in the house came out onto his back porch. The house was raised off the ground like mine, so I immediately suspected he had a basement similar to mine. It was an old house, for sure.

"May I help you, ma'am?" the man asked.

"No, I'm sorry. I didn't mean to intrude. I thought I saw someone I knew come into your yard. I must have been mistaken. Please pardon my intrusion," I answered, a bit taken aback by the whole scenario.

I guessed the man to be two or three years older than I and immediately wondered why he was still here. He only lived a block away from me, but I had never seen him before.

"It's no problem at all. I'm rather pleased to meet you. I've heard good things about you," the man answered.

I stopped in my tracks and stared at him. "What do you mean? Do I know you?" I asked. My eyes squinted to tiny slits as I peered at this rather handsome stranger.

Questions raced through my mind, and I'm sure my breath quickened. I wasn't sure if it was fear that pierced my consciousness or simply curiosity mixed with a bit of intrigue.

"Probably not, but I have heard about your teaching. You taught one of my nieces a while back, a little blond named Natasha. Do you remember her?" the man asked.

My entire body tensed. I chose my words carefully. My curiosity was rapidly turning to fear. "Why yes, I do remember her. She is quite brilliant. Where is she now?" I asked. If he knew about Natasha, just how much did he know about me?

The tall man looked around the yard and peered carefully at me, as if he were sizing me up and deciding how much to trust me. "She is living in Amsterdam and going to the university. Would you like to have a seat on that bench for a few minutes?" he asked.

His eyes darted around the green enclosure, and he hesitated as he stepped off the porch and walked toward me. He obviously could see the fear in my face. He smiled and put one finger to his lips, indicating I should not speak. He pointed toward an old wooden bench that had obviously been built before the intricate wrought iron benches became the standard.

he bench was weathered but welcoming,

unlike the cold iron. A weeping willow hung over the bench, almost touching the silver wood. I could smell the green smell of a garden mixed with dew that lingered from the morning because of the shade produced by the lush foliage enclosing the cozy garden. Something about the scene spelled mystery.

I thought this very strange, but instinct moved me in the direction of the bench. I cast him a look of suspicion, but the expression must have had a hint of trust in it. Something about his eyes mesmerized me. His gesture indicated caution, and I guessed what he was cautioning me about. It was almost as if I were reading his mind and he mine.

He pointed to the bench in the far corner of the simple garden where flowers bloomed in profusion beneath the willow tree. He followed silently, holding aside the friendly white daisies, as I walked toward the bench then sat down after he brushed a few fallen leaves from the smooth wood with his hand.

This mysterious man had the long slender fingers of a musician, but instinctively, I knew this was not his gift. He sat down beside me and glanced toward the gate where the man had come into the enclosure. The gate was now closed, and I was certain I had not closed it behind me. His body was only inches from mine. I could feel heat from his arm near mine. We sat there several minutes before he said anything. He glanced furtively around the park-like enclosure constantly.

"I apologize for being so secretive, but I must not be heard speaking of Natasha. I think you might guess why not. No one can hear us when we speak in this particular spot."

At this point, I was completely confused, but something told me to trust this stranger. Normally, I trust no one, not even Lillian. "Do I know you?" I asked. I squinted in the late afternoon sun as I turned my face upward toward his. I was struck by his eyes. They were like seawater crystals, not quite blue, but not really green either. I couldn't look away from his face.

He said, "No, but I know quite a bit about you. The official answer about Natasha is that she is studying in Amsterdam with her twin sister. I don't think you ever taught Natalie. She is quite a different character than her sister. Natasha took to you quite readily."

"And I to her. She seemed to understand the gravity of our *situation*. I assume that means she isn't actually in Amsterdam?" I asked in a whisper. I cocked my head to the side and looked up at the man sitting beside me with thinly veiled curiosity. He was not handsome in the usual sense, but he had magnetism about him. His hair was thick and streaked with white. It curled about his ears and at the nape of his neck. His shoulders were broad and thick, but he was rather slender and moved with strength and grace, almost without seeming to move at all. "Do you mind telling me your name before we go on with this mystery?"

The man laughed and said, "I'm Bjorn, Natasha's uncle. Natasha's mother is my sister."

"Oh, that explains part of this scenario. So are you going to tell me where Natasha actually is?"

"Yes, I am. I think it might interest you. No one else knows her actual whereabouts except her parents and sister. You see, her twin, Natalie, is attending the university under two separate identities, hers and Natasha's. In two more years, Natasha will have a degree in art history just like her sister, but she will most likely still not be able to tell a Rembrandt from a Holbein. Minor problem. The good thing is that Natasha will be able to decode messages and do wonders with AI. You see, that is my field. I'm guessing you might realize that I am past the magic age of 65."

"Yes, I thought you might be. How did you get a dispensation to stay here?" I asked. I looked up at him and realized he had a significant scar on his left cheek. I focused on his heavy silver gray eyebrows and unusual eyes but kept noticing the scar twitch when he mentioned Loki.

"I appear to be quite a help to Commissar Loki, so he has allowed me to stay on working for him until he deems me no longer useful. I'm sure he would have replaced me if he had been able to, but so far he has no one with my skills. I went to college before the curriculum was *improved*, so I have an actual education, which makes me essential to him. I assure you, he isn't keeping me because he loves my company. If he weren't so arrogant, he would fear me, as he should," said Bjorn. His scar moved but stopped twitching when he smiled. The shadows of a low-hanging limb of the willow darkened his face temporarily causing him to look even more mysterious.

"Wow! I'm stunned that you pulled that off. I have a feeling he should fear you. I certainly hope I don't need to do the same. I'm trying to get a dispensation to stay on and teach, but I don't think that will happen. I don't think Loki is going to allow me to stay beyond my birthday, but more importantly, where is Natasha?"

"Oh, you will see her again. She actually lives in my basement. I have one very much like yours. Yes, I know about your basement. I know a lot about you that you don't realize. You might say I'm 'home-schooling' Natasha at this point. Her parents live in Europe now, but she wanted to stay here, so she is with me. She's quite interested in science, so there is much I can teach her. I don't think the university is right for her now. You could say, she 'dropped out' for a while. Would you like to come in for a cup of tea?" Bjorn offered.

I was puzzled and a bit uneasy, but decided

to take him up on his offer. I knew I didn't have a lot more time in Ragnarock, so it really didn't matter anyway. "Yes, that would be nice. Thank you. Are we safe to go inside and talk?" I asked as we walked across the damp grass. Bjorn held a long stemmed sunflower aside as I ducked under it. He smiled but did not answer me. We reached the back steps and I noticed the tell-tale signs of the basement foundation. The old steps creaked as I put my foot on the first one as if it were warning me. We were both silent as we entered the house.

Bjorn held the oaken screen door open, and I entered into a world of the past. Dishes sat in a drain beside a spotless porcelain sink. Cupboards were stocked with flowered plates and glasses of different colors, turned on their tops in two neat rows of four each. The cupboard doors were antique glass and allowed full view of their contents but gave the glasses a surreal appearance because of the wave pattern molded into the glass. The cupboards were strikingly similar to mine but the contents were different. Almost all of the houses on this street were built around the time mine was built one hundred years ago, but most had been remodeled or razed, unlike mine and this one. Both were anachronisms as were their inhabitants.

"Please come in. I apologize for not introducing myself sooner. This was my family's home before they went to Paradise Valley. I was able to get a dispensation to stay here and work a bit longer. You see, I am in the electronics field, and my work has some benefit to the Commissar's office. Our work is quite complex, but I enjoy being of benefit to my community," Bjorn said, but before I could answer, he put a finger to his lips as he had done in the garden. He held his hand up as a stop sign.

Instantly, I understood. I stood still and mute while Bjorn left the room. He went into what appeared to be a closet. As I stared at the door, I smiled at the change in Bjorn's tone when he was inside the house. I looked out the window at the back fence and wondered where Uncle Miko had gone and what happened to him. I was sure now that I actually had seen him although he had been "dead" for many years.

Bjorn came out after five minutes or so and said, "My dear Yona, I suspect that you know why I left the room and why I said what I did. We may now speak freely. I am able to jam the devices for a short period of time. They believe I jam them so I can use all the power of my equipment to work on a project, so I cannot leave them off for long. You may have guessed by now that I know the man who came through my back yard."

"Was that my Uncle Miko?" I asked.

"Yes, it was."

"But I thought he was killed years ago," I

said, although I was not at all surprised to hear he was alive.

"That is what most people believe, but I assure you, he is alive and well. At the ripe old age of 85, he still has more brain power than the rest of us combined. He is the most brilliant man I have ever known. In my small circle, we refer to him as The Hammer. He is mythical in his power. Please sit down, Yona. We have very little time so I need to explain," Bjorn told me.

He continued, "I cannot tell you where he lives, but he is alive and well, although he is getting on in age. He was so feared by those in power that they attempted to have him eliminated. That's how I got this scar," Bjorn said as he rubbed his hand across the scar on his face. "They believed the train had run over him. One of Loki's henchmen got off a shot at me. It merely grazed my face, and he was never able to identify me. They know someone was with Miko that day, but they don't know who it was. Since that day, he has waged a war I don't think we can win. He lives alone with a gray wolf and a powerful bank of devices I have helped smuggle to him. I am able to communicate with him at certain times. He was here today to get some supplies he needed. He should not have left the garden, but he was looking for you. He escaped through a tunnel under the garden hedge. It has been there for nearly 100 years. It was part of another era and another cause. It was actually part of an elaborate bomb shelter during the cold war."

"I'm overwhelmed. I don't know what to say. Will I get to see him?"

"I don't know, but we must get you a dispensation. You cannot get on that train, no matter what we have to do. We have been working on a plan for the past year. You cannot go! Not yet anyway. We have a plan to save you, but we cannot move on it yet. I have connections and have some influence over Loki. We are manipulating some data now and will make it difficult for your department to find a replacement for you. We are stalling for time. Trust me. You must go now. My time is almost up. Leave by the back steps and exit to your left. Go around the magnolia tree and out the back gate."

"Bjorn, my friend Lillian is going to be 65 on the 15th of March. Is there any way for me to stop her from getting on the train?"

"No, I'm afraid not. I'm sorry."

I tensed up and I'm sure my face turned red. My eyes closed and my chin dropped. Bjorn pulled me to him and put his arms around me. He held me close and whispered in my ear, "I'm sorry."

His scent lingers with me still. It is one I will never forget. I am sorry I did not find him earlier in my life. If I never see him again, I know I will remember the way he smelled for the rest of my life. It was a magnet, one I had never felt before. I realized he was a man, clean, simple, and powerful.

I looked up at him and knew he truly was sorry. "You must go now," he said quietly, but he hesitated to release me for a long moment.

"She won't survive, will she?" I asked as I pulled away from him.

Bjorn took a deep breath and slowly shook his head. His eyes couldn't meet mine.

I turned my face away from him and walked quietly out the door. I closed the door without a sound and walked through the high grass, feeling the moisture on my ankle where the elephant had scraped it. I shivered. Once outside the garden, I quickened my pace and reached my house before my thoughts could unscramble themselves. I walked up my back steps with my head held high, but tears wet my face where it had recently lain on Bjorn's chest.

My key turned in the lock, and I stepped inside. When the lock clicked shut, I leaned against the door and clapped my hand over my mouth to stifle a scream rising deep inside my heart. I leaned against the cold door to keep myself from collapsing. I slowly slid down the surface until I was sitting on the hard floor. I couldn't cry—I could barely breathe. My worst fears about Paradise Valley had been confirmed. I was about to lose my closest life-long friend, and I could not even tell her. I knew I could not watch her board that train. I would have to go on about my business every day and say nothing.

It was long into the night when I finally got up. My breathing had almost returned to normal. I began trying to make sense of what I had learned earlier in the day. I had so many questions and no one to answer them. I went into the basement looking for answers.

I have always been able to find answers in books, in stories, but tonight I have so many new questions and few answers. I leafed through novels and articles from the past until my eyes fastened on the 2009 article concerning the new bioethics. I read it more carefully than ever before: the answer stared back at me from the faded type on the yellowed page. Suddenly I know what is happening.

Reality is now a locomotive ramming at full speed into my life. It cannot be stopped. Loki has supreme control at this point. I still have a hand gun and a long rifle hidden in the basement, but that would only get me killed. Loki has more firepower than anyone knows about. He is a three-headed snake and can strike in all directions. I feel utterly helpless. I might be able to kill Loki, but I would die in the process, and that will not save Lillian. Bjorn says I cannot save her, but I am not ready to give up. I could try to reason with her and get her a dispensation, but she will never allow that. She won't believe me even if I give her the facts (if I actually knew all the facts).

Still, there is my own dispensation to worry about, and how about Uncle Miko? That mystery is driving my imagination to new heights. Where is Uncle Miko? If only I could talk to him and ask him what to do. I am sure he knows the truth.

They know he knows the truth—that's why he isn't safe. They are aware that there is nothing more dangerous than a man—or a woman—who knows the truth and isn't afraid to die.

And Bjorn, what is his role in all this? With all these questions on my mind and no sleep for the past 36 hours, I am dressing for work and leaving my house at the usual time and in the usual manner. Nothing, however, seems real or *usual* anymore.

January 25, 2050

After my first class, Nicoli remained at his desk after the others had left. He was scribbling on a piece of white paper and did not look up. I walked casually over to his desk and stood behind him watching his pen strokes over his shoulder. His marks on the paper were a fine form of French script handwriting, which no one can read in 2050. He had written a question: "Are you ok?"

"Nikoli, that is a fine drawing you have made. Could I make a suggestion?" I asked.

"Certainly, Professor," Nikoli answered.

I wrote in the same elaborate script, "Yes, just a bit unnerved. I will explain later. Go on to class. I think I am going to leave early today, but I can't meet with you for the next month. It will be ok. I just need some time to work out my dispensation so that I can stay a bit longer. Please tell the others." I looked at Nikoli and smiled, but there was no heart in the smile.

Nikoli readily recognized that fact. He returned my disingenuous smile and got up to leave. On the way out, he slipped the note into the shredder. The shredder ground to a stop and reminded me how ancient I am. Shredders were no longer necessary because all information was kept in computer banks, not on paper. Paper was only used for artwork.

I should drop my effort to get a dispensation so that Bjorn could pursue his efforts. I don't want to bring suspicion to his efforts. I will pretend to be contented. Every breath in me feels like a lie, but truth in this case will not set me free. It will get me killed.

I think my days are numbered, so why does it matter? I don't have an answer to that question. Still somehow I know it does matter. Each day seems like an eternity—maybe it is my eternity. Dear diary, I hear Bjorn's voice. Where is he…? I don't see him, but I hear him.

"Just be patient," he is saying. Oh my God!

Have I lost my mind? I know he isn't here. I locked the door but I hear him. I know I hear him.

7

BENEATH A WANING MOON

January 26, 2050

Dear Diary,

It is the wee hours of the morning. Sleeping
has become a lost art for me. I cannot sleep. The
voice I heard was Bjorn's, but he was not here. I
have read about the connection some people can
have, brain-to brain, but I have never experienced it
before. I am sure it was Bjorn talking to me, but he
was not with me. Physicists say it is an electronic
connection some brains have. They say it even
exists after the body dies. No one has been able to
harness it, but I believe it is real. Bjorn's voice told
me to remain quiet. He says his plan is working and
that I am to go on as if I were planning to catch that
wretched train in August, but he says I will not be
on the train. He has a plan and Uncle Miko is going

to take me away to a safe place. But where??? I have no idea. He didn't tell me anything about Paradise Valley, but I sense death, I see smoke, and I smell gas. I've checked all my gas connections here in my house, and nothing is wrong. I have the most awful feeling, but I don't understand. His voice is soothing. It is deep and strong. I must see him…and Natasha, I need to talk to her. She must be in danger. I will slip down the alley and creep through the bamboo hedge before dawn.

Later….I went to see Bjorn. It was a dark night. The clouds were heavy over the city and the smell of gas is still with me. It seems to be permanently embedded in my clothes, even in my hair. Sometimes we have days like this when the smell is so heavy. No one knows why. The scientists tell us the climate control devices sometimes malfunction. I think that is bullshit.

They know what is happening and maybe I know too. Bjorn knows…I'm sure of that, but he won't tell me. I'm beginning to be able to read his thoughts as well. He doesn't like that. I can tell. He doesn't know I write all this down. He would most likely tell me to destroy you, dear diary, but I won't. Perhaps this is my final act of defiance.

They are going to kill me anyway, so why not? I got to the gate just before dawn and eased it open without a sound. My thoughts and fears must have woken Bjorn because he came out the back door in his shorts and without a shirt or shoes. For an old man, he has a remarkably toned body, not that I noticed, of course.

He saw me right away and swore. "Damn, Yona! What are you doing here? I told you not to come," he whispered as I reached the back steps.

"In case you aren't aware, I am not very good at taking orders. And how did you send that message to me? I've never experienced that before," I answered.

"Mental telepathy. You've never experienced it before?"

"No, have you?"

"Yes, Miko and I have communicated like that for years. I wasn't sure you would hear me. But I told you not to contact me."

"Why not?"

"Because Loki does not need to know I am helping you! If he does, your cause is doomed. He is suspicious of me and only keeps me because he needs me. I've heard he is ill, so maybe there is hope. You can bet your ass he isn't going to "ride the magic carpet" to Paradise Valley though…he's special. He's special alright. I've never known anyone as evil as he is. Unfortunately he is extremely intelligent, but he's not quite as smart as he thinks he is. They never are. Get in the house before someone sees you."

I walked in the house and he pointed toward

the basement and put his finger to his lips again. He pulled back a bookcase, exposing an opening to a set of stairs. He passed his hand over a plate on the wall and the stairs lit up. I walked down behind him to a small room with a table and a bank of computers along one wall. He directed me to a chair beside him and began clicking keys without touching them.

He said, "Natasha is sleeping so we need to be quiet but here is what I'm doing." Then he showed me the applications of people who had applied for my position. I saw him erase some information in one and supplant it with facts that would cause the application to be rejected immediately. I smiled and he turned the machine off.

The room was dimly lit. The one lamp lit the side of his face with the scar. Something about it touched me, and I put my hand on the scar. Bjorn smiled and looked at me without blinking. "Thank you," I said.

"For what?" he answered.

"For saving Uncle Miko and for trying to help me."

"It's far more than that, Yona. There aren't many of us left. Have you ever read *The Time Machine*?"

"Of course, it's one of my favorite books."

"I guessed as much. We are being eaten by

the Morlocks, my dear. Don't you realize that? If we don't try to save the few of us who can still see clearly, no one has a chance."

What did he mean by that? I'm still not sure, but I stood so close to him I could feel his breath against my skin. The air around us seemed to be pushing me closer to him, but he stood like a statue in front of me. The seriousness of his statement felt like a vice closing in on me, but even that fear could not stop my thoughts at that moment. Bjorn never took his eyes off me. Then the heavy air shattered like glass when he spoke.

"You know I can read your thoughts, don't you?" Bjorn said.

I think I must have blushed because if he could read my thoughts at that moment, I would be embarrassed. Apparently he did. He penetrated the bubble trapping me inside. He kissed me tenderly at first then with passion. The walls of time came down with a crash that still echoes in my brain.

"Still embarrassed?" he asked.

"Yes," I answered.

"Why? I know exactly what you are thinking."

I raised my eyebrows and backed up a few inches from his face. "This just isn't like me," I tried to explain.

"Don't you realize I know that?" he asked as he laughed at me.

Ironically, I was not offended. "I suppose you do. That makes things simpler, doesn't it?"

"Yes, it does—but infinitely more complicated at the same time. I've watched you for years, but it seemed very impractical for me to reveal my presence to you. Loki cannot learn of my connection to Miko or all our efforts will be for nothing. We must be very discreet and not meet in person again. I will talk to you through MT. When you want to talk to me, go to your basement and sit in the blue chair in the corner of the room between the last two book cases. That is where I saw you, and knew I could communicate with you yesterday. I will sit here in this chair. Let's do that at midnight each night, and we will be able to hear each other perfectly, but no one else will be able to pick up our communication. Very few have this ability anyway, but none can pick it up when we are in these two specific locations."

I blinked after staring at him as he spoke. "Okay. This is quite a large pill for me to swallow all at once. Can Natasha do this also?"

"No, she can't. I can't do it with her mother either. Not many can."

"How did you learn to do this?"

"Miko taught me."

"I should have figured that. Then why can't you teach Natasha?"

"I tried. She doesn't have the gene. Only a

very few have the gene, and only if you have the gene and you are fortunate enough to find your Yoda, can you use it. Miko thought I might have it, so he tried to communicate with me, and it worked. At first I didn't know why I was having these strange insights that were so like his, but then he told me and taught me how to reciprocate. He's been my mentor for many years. He told me about you long before I saw you. I think he always intended us to be together. He told me you have the power also, but I might have to teach you. He wasn't sure he would ever see you again, but he knew I would find you. He told me he knew you had the gift the day you were born when he first looked into your eyes."

"Well that explains a lot of things. Do you think I can communicate with him if I try? I think he's been communicating with me for years. I just didn't recognize it for what it was."

"He has been reading your thoughts for years. And I'm sure he's been sending you some of his, but he guards many of his thoughts with an iron shield, not literally, of course, but he keeps much of his mind to himself for fear that others might be endangered. He would never want you to be harmed by knowing too much. Knowing too much in our world is very dangerous. Unfortunately, knowledge here does not make you free. It often results in an early trip to Paradise.

"Somehow I knew that. I've always kept my thoughts mostly to myself, not knowing why. At least I thought I was keeping them to myself. Apparently I wasn't. Strangely, I feel some kind of relief knowing that you and Uncle Miko can read my thoughts. Wait…can he read what I'm thinking right now?"

Bjorn laughed and pulled me so close to him that I could feel his heart beating. "He won't mind."

For the first time since my parents died, I felt safe in an ultimately unsafe world. Safe and warm, very warm. My body was suddenly limp but I didn't sink to the floor because Bjorn held me so tightly to him. He knew what I was experiencing. He rested his cheek against my head and slowly stroked my back.

"You will be safe."

"For some strange reason, I believe you." I don't think I said the words but rather felt them, as did he.

With my head still comfortably nestled into his chest, I asked, "How did Natasha's family get out of here, and how did they get permission for her to attend the university in Amsterdam?"

Bjorn released me from his embrace and looked at my face when he said, "As you know, her father is a physician. He is involved in some very sophisticated research into the malady that will eventually claim Loki's life. I am not sure what that malady is because I don't have training in that field, but I understand it is some complicated disease process involving his liver. Loki, of course, wants immortality if at all possible and definitely wants to live as long as possible. He allowed Natasha's family to go so that her father could learn methods to cure him. Everything with him is a selfish motive. His ego exceeds all bounds." Bjorn laughed and added, "Of course, he isn't interested in going to Paradise Valley."

"Wow! I would have never guessed any of that…except Loki's ego and his avoidance of Paradise Valley, of course. I could guess that."

Bjorn laughed again and the scar wrinkled. "Now, go! You must go home before dawn. We can't let you go to the Valley of Death. Go!" he said to me.

I was at the same time amused and terrified! He actually called it the Valley of Death. So I am right in my assumption. I smiled a somewhat limp smile at him and paused. I stood there long enough for him to lean down and kiss me one more time. Then I smiled for real. I slipped back up the stairs and through the bookcase then out through the back garden hedge.

I am terrified but at the same time, happier than I have ever been. I may have only seven months to live, but I sense a change in the way I will live those short months. So here I am in the blue chair again writing in my diary. Uhoh! You know what I'm writing, don't you.

"Yes," the voice answered. It seemed to be audible, but I knew it wasn't. "Is that ok with you?" Yes, I suppose it will have to be. But I think I kind of like it.

February 14, 2050

Oh, my goodness, Dear Diary. Bjorn is the most amazing man. He is brilliant. So far none of the applicants for my job have been accepted. I have not seen him for more than two weeks. My heart begs me to go back to his house, but so far, my brain is winning that battle. I just wish I could communicate with Uncle Miko like I do with Bjorn. I don't think that can happen, but Bjorn says I have the gift and Uncle Miko communicates with me. I understand those MT communications are rare, and apparently I don't have it with anyone else. Maybe that's for the best that Uncle Miko can't hear me, at least for the present.

"But I can, my dear." The voice was tender and deep. "Believe what Bjorn tells you. He will bring you to me when the time comes. We will keep you safe. Trust him and do as he says. Don't question too much. You will hear from me when you need to, but it is best for you to trust us and remain quiet."

I looked around me and realized the room

was still and silent. Those words had been totally in my head. Am I becoming schizophrenic? If I tell anyone what I'm experiencing, Loki will surely have me locked up and sent away to Paradise. I hear laughter and I look up. I have no idea what I'm looking for. Oh my God, am I losing my mind? I hear the laughter again but this time it is clearly Bjorn laughing at me. Damn it! What is happening?

"Happy Valentine's Day, Yona. Yes, it's me. Come to me just before dawn. Come in the back door. I will be waiting and the door will be unlocked. Come to the basement."

Dear Diary, what do I do now? Am I losing my mind completely? Do I go and make a complete fool of myself? Sure I do. We both knew the answer to that before I wrote the words.

February 15, 2050: 4:00 am

I closed my door without a sound and slipped out the back and down the alley toward Bjorn's house. The grass was wet and I could feel moist leaves brush my legs as I walked. The alley was rarely used so it had grown up with weeds, some with flowers. White moonshade blossoms hung over my path creating a sort of eerie light. They looked like lanterns with their pollen-covered wicks extending into the darkness.

Suddenly a gray cat darted across the path in front of me. It was as if he couldn't see me. He paused listening for a mouse he must have heard. He appears not to see me at all. Am I really here? What is happening to me? Am I Alice in wonderland? Holy Hell, Toto, we're not in Kansas anymore! The cat lunged into the bushes and I heard a small squeak then thrashing and finally, chomping.

I kept walking as if in my sleep. In my dream. That's what this is: I'm dreaming. But no, I wasn't dreaming. I walked on, one step at a time until I reached Bjorn's door. Just as he had said, it was unlocked. I went in and locked the door securely behind me. The only sound was the slow snap of the latch. I pulled the bookcase aside and inched down the steps. When I reached the bottom step he was waiting, smiling. The lamp lit the scar. I reached out to touch his face. I touched the scar.

"Yes, it is real. I am real. Natasha is sleeping. We can go into my study."

I followed him, not asking what was happening. It was all too unreal to question. He opened the door to a room I had not seen before. It had no windows and seemed to be cooler that the other rooms. I shivered.

"You are safe here. If you have to disappear, this is where you will come. This room is dug into the earth and sealed. No communication can penetrate these earthen walls, nor can any words escape."

I stared at him with questions racing through my brain.

"No, you are completely sane. This is happening, I promise you." Bjorn sat down on a large sofa and patted the seat beside him. I sat like an obedient child beside him. Then he spoke to me in a voice that felt like a summer wind. I could almost hear wind chimes in the background. "Yona I know you are afraid, but I need you to trust me. I will do everything I can to keep you safe, but we both know that might not be enough. No one is safe in our world, but you are definitely not crazy." He smiled at me, but the corners of his mouth turned down slightly. I knew what the smile meant. I felt it.

Bjorn turned my face to meet his, then he kissed me with a fire I had never known before. I put my arms around him and pulled him so close to me I could feel his heart beating. His kisses moved to my shoulders then he moved his body away from mine and looked into my eyes. I felt as if I were hypnotized. He unbuttoned first the top button of my shirt then the second. He began to kiss my neck then inched down. Then the shirt came off and he stood up. I followed him and smiled looking at him. I knew every thought that passed through his brain as he did mine.

He tossed the cushions of the sofa to the floor. I dropped to my knees on the first cushion. For a long moment, he stood over me like a colossus in a dream. He smiled and I smiled. The only thought I remember is one of wonder. He is extremely toned for a man in his late 60's.

Everything from that moment seemed as real as life could be, far more real than anything I had ever experienced before. If I am crazy, then I hope I never recover. I had two brief affairs when I was young, but what I experienced today just before dawn was nothing like that. I have finally connected with another human being. This was more real than any second of my life. Lying beside him on the floor of this man-made cave, feeling completely relaxed, I believed him when he told me he would never leave me. Whatever happens to us, will happen to both of us. He propped up on one elbow and looked at my face. He smiled.

"Yona, I've wanted to do that most of my adult life. I've loved you from a distance for so long. I will do whatever must be done to make sure I never lose you. We will have to be apart for a while, at least until I can talk to Miko. He will help me find a way for us to be together. I have to get your deferment first to give us more time. Now I know what I'm fighting for, and I will fight until I win—until we win. Miko and I will work together. I don't know if we can ever bring Loki down, but we will do that if we can, and if not, we will escape together. Either way, I will always be a part of you from now until eternity. I promise you that."

I believed him without question. I believe him and believe my world is real now. I understood a lot about life at that moment, how one human can be one with another. I trust now. I didn't answer him with words, but he could see my thoughts in my face, and he could hear the unspoken words in my brain. I love him without reservation, and I trust him.

He lay back down beside me and stared at the low ceiling. I read every thought that went through his head. His thoughts were a stew of many flavors. He was planning and some of his plans involved great danger, but I sensed no fear in him, only determination. Loki has met his match. Bjorn is tall and strong, but his strength lies more in his mind than his body. He stood up and reached his hand down to me. I took his hand without a word and began putting my clothes on. He did the same. We didn't need to touch, we didn't need to talk. Each of us knew where we were going.

When we were dressed, he kissed me once more then said, "Go home and go to work today just as usual. Keep a low profile while I work on your papers. You know I want you to come back again, but that should not happen, as much as we both want it. It will come later, but right now we cannot let our feelings jeopardize our future together. We must understand our mission and do whatever we have to do."

"I understand," I said to him. I walked back up the stairs, opened the door and disappeared back down the alleyway. The moonshade blossoms had begun to close with the rising sun. They bowed their heads as if in sorrow, but their delicate fragrance lingered like a fog in my path. Every time I smell the moonshade blossoms from this day forward, I will think of Bjorn, but when do I not think of him?

March 15, 2050

Time is drizzling away. I have not been back down the alley past the moonshade since that night, the night with Bjorn. I know his warning is correct. He knows my fears about Lillian. I talk to him every night from the blue chair, but that is no longer enough.

Lillian refuses to be persuaded as March 15th looms. I have spent less and less time with her. Looking into her eyes has become unbearable. I know I cannot influence Lillian, and I know what will happen to her today. Well, I don't know in reality, but I know I will never see her again, and I know her life will not be peaches and cream after the Ides of March.

We have become a bit estranged, so I don't know what she has been thinking, but today I received a message from her. It ended abruptly, as I suspect, did her life. I may never know the circumstances of her final demise, but I know she is gone. Here is what she told me:

"I woke up this morning with all the excitement of a five year old on Christmas morning. I thought of it as Christmas coming early this year. Life has been dragging along for me for the last few years since Fred left on the Magic Carpet. We had been close friends since we started elementary school, but I never knew how much I loved him until I waved to him as the train pulled away from the station. I couldn't put my finger on it, but something was wrong that day. I had one of "those feelings." Something wasn't right. I understood why they let him go on ahead of me, but my heart hurt so much when the train pulled away with him aboard.

You know I got the highly anticipated message from him that night, so I thought he was happy and enjoying his new home, but deep inside my heart, I knew something wasn't right. We have messaged each other every Saturday night since he transitioned, but I never really felt like he was the same old Fred. He was definitely different. His memory seemed sound. He remembered every childhood shenanigan we had participated in and he knew all about me and about our life together, but he seemed robotic.

I began to wonder if he was just pretending to be happy. I thought he would be happy again soon though because we would be together again. I planned to give him the biggest hug ever when I stepped off that train and ran to him.

I was really looking forward to seeing him again that night when I arrived in Paradise Valley. He had told me he'd be waiting at the station when I arrived and would take me home. He said I would share his apartment with him. He said it was a lovely place and he had recently had my kitchen repainted with my favorite color: yellow. He said he'd even planted some huge sunflowers that bloomed continuously throughout the year. They were just outside the window. I could imagine the happy flowers and the tiny blue birds that would gather the seeds as they ripened. You remember the blue birds, I'm sure.

I dressed for the journey with a smiling face. It would be the trip of a lifetime. And to think…it was all free, well, not quite free. Fred and I had been paying half our paychecks each week into the system all our lives so we could take this journey. Nevertheless, I thought it would be perfect. I trusted that it would because Fred had told me all about it. I dreamed about it the night before, so I woke up with a big smile. Today is the day, I thought. I would finally see Fred again today, but now I'm beginning to wonder if you might be right. You might be, but it is too late.

I'm already on the train and I know they won't let me get off. I'm not even sure I want to get off. What would happen if I did? Yona, I'm scared for the first time in my life. Oh my God, what have I done?

I was a bit disappointed that you were not here to see me off, but you have become distant recently, so I wasn't really surprised. Now I'm beginning to suspect why. Something is wrong—I can sense it. I feel the train beginning to move. Everyone on the train is silent. Something is wrong. I know it is.

As always, those lovely, cheerful signs instructed us birthday folks and a few early arrivals to line up and board when their number was called. 'Number 451, board at this time and have your card stamped at the door,' I heard them say, so I stepped up into the train.

Just before I boarded, I turned on my device so I could send you this last message. I hope there will be many more over time, but now I'm not sure. I suppose you will find out later what happened to me. I just hope I get to see you in August and all my fears are for nothing. Oh, Yona, don't ride the magic carpet—find a way to get out of this. I just know this is not good. I love you, my dear good friend.

The door slid open without a sound and I stuck my preprinted and perforated card into the slot. The heavenly scent of lavender floated in the air above the seats. I breathed deeply and closed my eyes for a moment anticipating the end of the journey when I can once again put my arms around Fred. Something about the odor in the train is relaxing me.

The difference between us is that you always seem to know where you are going and I don't. Somehow this time is different. I'm afraid today. I'm dreadfully afraid you have been right all along. The gooey sweet voice in the train is speaking now: 'Welcome aboard the Paradise Valley Express, your magic carpet ride to the next life,' it is saying. I obediently took my seat. You know I always obey the rules.

Of course there is no driver. There haven't been any drivers in years. All the engineers have to do is preprogram the route and the train delivers the passengers precisely at the correct time to the desired destination point. No human assistance is needed for the journey, especially this journey.

What a Godsend I thought these new fangled inventions were! I couldn't imagine how the poor early humans had survived without them. Now I'm wishing there was a driver I could shout at. I would tell him to STOP and let me off!

Soon the train filled with excited seniors anxious to get this journey started. Like me, they thought it would be the best time of their lives. Some of them probably still think that. They are chattering and laughing, but I'm not! After working so many years, they believe they can finally relax and enjoy life. My naiveté allowed me to enjoy the thought of this journey, but I know you did not share the same thoughts. Somehow, I know now that you probably were right. Something is wrong!

A second train following us turned onto a track heading north. I am wondering if this was the train to Nirvana. A twinge of jealousy tingled in my brain for just a moment then I thought about Fred. He's waiting for me. So I shouldn't be jealous. I have Fred…or do I? Surely he's waiting for me.

The ride through the countryside would have been most pleasant if not for my growing fears. I've never seen much of this landscape. I'm beginning to relax a little. I guess I was just afraid of the unknown. Maybe you are wrong.

We finally arrived at the gates of the Paradise Valley Hotel. Just like at the station, signs directed our path. We flocked in like a bunch of sheep, taking it all in. The hotel seemed to be the only building for miles and miles. That seemed odd, but at least I thought we would have privacy here and miles of gorgeous ground for long walks. Maybe the apartments are at another location and we will be transported there later…after the induction ceremony.

Oh my God, where is Fred? He said he would be waiting. I don't see anyone walking about outside the hotel, so that must be the case. He'll be waiting when we are delivered to the residences.

The hotel is constructed of the finest Italian marble and has a grand chimney; in fact, several chimneys rise above the roof. Smoke is coming from one of them, so I assumed this fantastic hotel has multiple fireplaces. You know I've always loved fireplaces. Now maybe I'll get my own.

Everyone is chattering excitedly. We are entering the elaborate hotel. Just like at the train station, there are no actual people here. All the "work" is done by robots, but the place is immaculate.

Roses are arranged beautifully in tall vases and the most heavenly scent floats through the vast room. The robots are directing us into the main dining hall. I wonder why Fred isn't here. He said he would meet me here, but I don't see him anywhere. Maybe he's waiting at our apartment. Surely he is.

Oh my God! Yona, the names of the dining rooms! Oh no! Yona, goodbye. I love you. The dining rooms are Auschwitz, Dachau, and Buchenwald. Why would they name dining halls with such names? Even though history classes no longer teach about those places, I remember my grandmother talking about them when I was very young. I know why. Oh my God! The robot is coming! He sees my device…I love you, Yona. The mist, Yona, the mist is dropping from vents in the ceiling….it's hissing—it's falling from vents in the ceiling. Oh my God—the chimneys..."

The message ended abruptly.

Oh, my God! It's even worse than I feared. Sweet Lilllian is gone. Now I know what Paradise Valley is. Never have I regretted being right more than I do at this moment. Bjorn must know and Uncle Miko—I'm sure he knows. That's why Loki tried to kill him. He knows.

March 16, 2050

I must see Bjorn. I must. I just received this text from Lillian: "My dearest Yona, I'm happy to tell you that Paradise Valley is all you could hope for. The flowers are just lovely and Fred sends his love. I am comfortably settled into our quarters. All our fondest wishes are satisfied here. Can't wait for you to join me."

The blue chair, I went to the blue chair when I got that message. Bjorn tried to calm me down. He said there was nothing I could do for Lillian. He said he was working on my deferral and that I should go on as usual. How can I do that…nothing is "usual" for me anymore. Time is running out. I know it is.

I know Bjorn is right. I must remain steadfast in my desire to keep working with my students. I have always managed to find a few whom I could pull aside and privately teach some of the now-discarded curriculum, like the dreaded lessons Lillian learned at the "Hotel." But I can no longer teach them without pain stabbing me in the heart.

Such urgency—but I must remain calm if I am to have any chance at all. I must not betray Bjorn. I must teach them, but they are doomed just like I am. I had applied for a "Special Circumstances" request to continue to work before I first spoke to Bjorn, so the Officer in charge of these requests contacted me and arranged an interview. Bjorn said I should go just as I had planned.

The interview would take place in the ominous looking structure overlooking the plaza where all club meetings take place. It was a lovely place when I was a teenager, but now even the pigeons have left for happier surroundings. I should meet with Bjorn before this interview. Perhaps he would be able to help. I do not want to get on that train. He has warned me about coming to his house, but this is an emergency, so I'm going.

I came out my back door just after nightfall wearing a black dress, sweeping to my ankles, hoping to blend into the night. The dress had a large collar I could use for a cowl to cover my hair. Draped accordingly, I shut the door quietly and looked to my left and right to be certain I was not attracting any undue attention. Slipping through the gap in the fence where the bamboo reeds serve as a gate, I disturbed an old owl. He hooted at me suggesting he knew more than I did. He perched in the old oak tree draping over the alley. Still I could see his amber eyes watching me as I moved past him. A briar snagged my dress and I yanked it loose. A strip of cloth clung to the briar. I looked back only once and saw the owl with yellow eyes cocking his head, watching the movement of the black flag left on the briar.

When I got to Bjorn's fence, I parted the reeds just enough to step through then let nature close the gate. Bjorn was standing at the window, looking for me. He opened the door without a sound as I stepped up onto the porch. He nodded toward the bookcase and went inside. I followed him to the bookcase then down the steps. Natasha was waiting at the small table. She had a book in front of her that had mysterious diagrams mapped out in front of her. She looked up at us as we came down the steps. She smiled.

"Hello, Dr. Maheegan, I was wondering when I would get to see you again. Uncle Bjorn tells me you want to postpone taking the ride. I can't say I blame you."

"Well, I'm very pleased to see you are in such capable hands. I understand you are learning to defeat the system."

"I hope so. I have another good teacher. I loved being in your classes. I hope you are still teaching."

"So far, I am still working with brilliant students like you, but I don't know how long that will last. I got a rather disturbing message last night, so the future seems very dim to me right now."

Bjorn pulled out a chair and motioned for me to sit across from Natasha. He remained standing at the end of the table. He asked. "So what exactly was it that you learned last night?"

"When Lillian got on the train to make her final journey, she somehow managed to turn on her device and message me. She confirmed all my worst fears." Tears started rolling down my cheeks and Bjorn came over to me.

"Natasha, could you give us some privacy?" he asked. Natasha nodded. She knew what happened to Lillian and so did Bjorn. Natasha also knew how stoic I try to be, so she understood perfectly what it was doing to me to fall apart. She disappeared and I collapsed. Bjorn held me until I stopped shaking then took me by the shoulders and held me away from him so he could look into my eyes.

"Yona, I know what happens to the happy crowds when they get to Paradise Valley. I was hoping you would not find out—at least not yet. I don't know how Lillian managed to get that message to you, but if Loki finds out, you will disappear—immediately. Give me your device and I will erase any trace of it. He can't find out—ever! Miko has managed to get close enough to the facility to find out exactly what happens. He's been trying to find a way to blow it up and stop the extermination process, but he hasn't been able to do it yet. We need more time, but our time is running out. He loves you so much, as do I. We are racing as fast as we can, but we need more time. We cannot let you go there. Right now, I think we would be in more danger to try to escape than we are to stand still where we are. I will get you a deferment. I have to!"

"Bjorn, where is Uncle Miko? I need to see him. Don't you understand that?"

"Yes, I do understand your need to talk to him, but right now, that is just too dangerous—for you and for him. Trust me."

"But what about my interview? The Commissioner's office contacted me and set up the appointment for my interview. What do I do about that?"

"You go, just as you have been requested. You go, but you don't tell them anything. You are a smart girl—play the game. I can assure you, you are smarter than the jerk conducting the interview. Even the interviewer most likely has no idea what happens to the people who go to Paradise Valley. He will go when his time comes just like all the other unsuspecting sheep. But you, my dear, will

NOT GO! I will give my life to keep that from happening."

"So you think, even Loki's people don't know?"

"Some of them do. They are the ones who ride the *second* train. They will never go to Paradise Valley. They have their own cushy setup. Miko has his eyes on it also. They have no idea how much danger they are actually in. Do you know the story of Thor and his legendary hammer?"

"Yes, I do. You are saying Uncle Miko has a hammer?"

"Yes, but not the conventional kind. His hammer is a bit more lethal."

"I remember he had a huge hammer in his workshop when I was a little girl, and he was very strong and could swing that hammer, but you don't mean that kind of hammer, do you?"

"No, I don't, but the analogy works. His hammer today fits the task he is faced with. He still has the power even though he is well into his eighties. He is a powerful man. Today his power comes from the brain, not the brawn. His brawn may be a little weakened by time, but his brain is stronger than ever. He swings a hammer even Loki should fear. He can sling the hammer he is working on now across many miles and hit his target with incredible precision. He can enter those lovely chimneys without even touching the bricks—and he will when the time comes. He hasn't quite perfected the technology to his satisfaction. At least he hadn't as of last week. So go to your interview and help us stall them just a few months, and we will bring Loki down."

"But what if you can't get me a deferral?"

"We will. We have to."

I looked at him and knew he would find a way. I asked him, "Is there any hope we can save Lillian?"

He looked away from me and said, "I think you know the answer to that."

I did. I didn't say anything else. I held him very close to me, letting his strength leach into me. His screen lit up and I knew it was time for me to go. I walked back up the steps without looking back. The owl was gone when I passed his perch again. I wondered if he would return or if it mattered.

My interview loomed. That might end it all for me. My appointment is April 25. Not much time to prepare. How do I prepare for a test when I don't know the subject matter? I'll talk to Bjorn every day, and I will keep going. Time will not stop for me as it did for Lillian. I hope.

8

CLOSE YOUR EYES WITH HOLY DREAD

April 25, 2050

  I am aware that the Commissar will have done his due diligence in investigating my background before the interview. I must be prepared to answer difficult questions and defend any mistakes I might have made along the way. Or better yet, I must prepare to defend things I've done right. Surveillance has improved significantly in the past twenty years, so cannot lie to the official interviewer.

  I will dress appropriately. I think I shall present myself in all white, like the angel I truly am. Blank, white, innocent—I am. I can look the part even if I can't ride the horse to the barn.

  Well, dear diary, here I go. White slacks,

white jacket, black (very sensible) shoes, hair controlled with disciplined precision. No wild red streaks lapping my eyebrows today. Lillian would laugh. "That's not you," she would say. Thinking of Lillian steels my backbone. I will not let them beat me like they did Lillian. Bastards! You'll see! More later after my visit to hell's minions.

The interview began very pleasantly. The Commissar's agent greeted me warmly, asking how my latest class was going and inviting me to sit in the lovely leather chair in front of his desk. However, before I sat down, I noted the cameras placed in each corner of the room. I smiled warmly at the agent and forcefully kept my voice in a steadily controlled monotone.

I channeled Eudora Welty's old Phoenix as she determined to complete her journey. I would keep going no matter what this jerk threw in my path. Bring on the rattlesnakes and briers. I'm ready. Most of the questions he asked were innocuous and did little more than to expose his incompetence, but finally he asked about a rally I attended during my senior year of college. It was a political rally for a now defunct party.

"Comrade Maheegan, I understand you attended a rally held at your university during your senior year. Is that information accurate?"

"Yes, it's been so long ago, I hardly

remember, but I think that is correct. All my friends were going, so I tagged along. You know how it is to want to be cool and not seem different," I said. This made me a bit uncomfortable, so I shifted slightly in my seat and sat up with my spine very straight.

The agent leaned back slightly in his chair and I heard the bolts squeak in one of the rollers. The agent had most definitely not missed any meals and the brass buttons on his jacket strained as he pressed the point. He tapped his pencil on the desk three times and rubbed his chin during the painfully long few seconds he hesitated looking for his next words. Finally he said, "You are aware, I assume, that the actions advocated by that party are the reasons it no longer exists. Do you feel society is better off without their interference?"

"Why, yes, certainly. We are obviously much safer without firearms, and I know rhetoric we heard about the free press that day was most definitely inciting the crowd. I don't believe I was aware of the intentions of the crowd when I agreed to attend." I stopped after that statement when I realized there was a strange sensation coming from the leather in the arm of the chair and a faint tapping sound was coming from a machine on the credenza behind the agent. I removed my arm from the armrest and folded my hands in my lap then the tapping stopped.

"And do you currently belong to any organizations?" the agent asked.

"No, I do not," I replied.

"Are you quite certain?" the agent said, looking directly into my eyes.

"Quite," I answered. I gave him the stink eye but veiled it so his ego allowed him to overlook it.

"Why have you removed your arms from the armrests of your chair?" he questioned again gazing directly into my eyes.

I stumbled a bit but managed to regain my composure and reply, "I don't know, sir. I have a slight shoulder problem and my arms were uncomfortable. Would you like me to put them back on the armrests?"

"No, that won't be necessary. You say you have a shoulder problem, then why are you requesting a dispensation to delay your departure to Paradise Valley?"

"It is very slight. I simply have to change the position of my arms and it abates. It does not interfere with my work. I get much pleasure from my work, so I would like to continue doing it."

"And Maheegan, is pleasure your goal in life. If so, Paradise Valley will provide much pleasure."

"No, I simply believe I have a lot to offer to the upcoming generation. I've been very successful in my teaching practice."

"And is it your belief that no one else can do that as well as you can?"

I had to take a deep breath before answering this. I realized my answer had to be the right one if I wanted the dispensation. Unfortunately, I wasn't quite sure what the right response was. I wanted to shout, "Yes, damn you! You are a pompous ass and don't know shit about what I do!" but I knew I could not. "No, Sir, I'm sure others could do as well, but I have many years of training and would appreciate a dispensation to use that training for a bit longer."

"Are there any other reasons you request this dispensation?"

"No, sir. That is it. I simply want to be useful to society."

I have so many more reasons, none of which he would understand. He only knew what he had been told. I could see that thinking was something he was not accustomed to doing. The more I talked the more chance I had to lose my bid, so I shut up—with much difficulty. It was not my way to stand silently when a voice needed to be heard. It never had been. I am a throwback to the days of my uncle, unfortunately.

The agent politely released me from the interview, but as I walked out, I saw him retrieve the tape from the ticking box on the credenza. I was more than surprised to see he still used such an archaic device. I had seen one of these decades ago on a detective show, so I recognized it immediately. I'm sure he had no idea I knew what it was. I walked across the parking lot and got into my car, but not before looking up at the agent's window. He was standing there watching me as I got in. I smiled at the stupid bastard. I knew he was too dense to get my message—at least I hoped he was. No finger gestures allowed.

The interview rattled me to the bone, but I would never allow it to show. I have to play the game. The stakes are now too high for me to fail. I'm not sure what it was, but something didn't seem right today. Well, I suppose I do know what it was, but I am clearly in uncharted and dangerous waters, and I know it.

I wanted to scream when I got into my car. It took everything in me to stifle my emotions and crank the car. I drove off as if nothing had happened. I wanted so much to voice all my thoughts to the smug bastard in the too-tight coat. But he was just an arm of the Kraken that had devoured sanity and personal liberty.

Angry and perplexed, I pulled over a few blocks away. I parked the car and tried to breathe deeply until I could still my racing heart. I took the pins out of my hair and shook it loose. I raked through it with my fingers and brought it back to its wild usual form.

Feeling a little more relaxed but still perplexed, I instructed the car to drive out to Apple Valley where my father grew up. I was counting on chance too much, but I just couldn't take one more minute in hell. We are cautioned not to drive into the countryside because of dangers there, but I perceived the dangers far more ominous where I was at the time. I had to escape if only for a brief time. Present dangers were the least of my worries.

Turning onto the overgrown lane gave me a special warm feeling. The pear trees in the distance were tangled with weeds and looked unkempt but they brought me back in time. Some of the anguish plaguing me began to dissipate. The air smelled green, fresh like new trees and spring flowers. Wild Confederate roses climbed into the trees and spread their pure white blossoms.

Only one old chimney and parts of a dilapidated barn remain on the property. No one lives there anymore, so I got out of my car and walked around to the back of the tumbled down barn. Suddenly I was aware that someone was watching me. The hair on the back of my neck stood up, but I didn't turn around. Then I heard steps behind me.

A deep, soft voice said, "You lost, Ma'am?"

I turned around to see Uncle Miko. He had always been the rebel in the family. He had been buried on the hill outside the town where unfortunates who met their demise before their time were deposited. It was clear to me at that moment that there were things I had grossly underestimated, even after talking to Bjorn and catching a glimpse of Miko fleeing Bjorn's garden. Seeing him standing near me brought the whole situation into full focus.

"Uncle Miko, I'm Yona, don't you remember me," I asked.

"Oh, Sweet Baby! Of course I do. You always were my favorite. It's just that it's been so long since I've seen you, and I didn't expect anyone to find me here."

"I'm confused, Uncle Miko. Bjorn told me you were alive and well, but he wouldn't tell me where you were. The Commissar told us you were killed by the train and were buried on the hill. Obviously that was highly exaggerated. How did you get here?

"Oh, sweet, innocent Yona, please, we must talk, but first bring your car around and park it in the barn so no one will see you. You are in danger by being here, but I have a feeling you know that or you wouldn't be here."

I nodded. I was confused but suddenly some errant pieces of the puzzle began to fall into place and the air felt right again. I tapped my device and obediently, my car cranked itself and steered flawlessly into the barn, then Uncle Miko eased the battered old barn door shut and locked the rusted lock. He said he had much to tell his favorite niece. This is what he told me today:

"I was twenty when you were born, but I knew when I saw you that you were special. I think it was some kind of special force that brought you here today. We must go down to the creek bank where we will be safe. There is a small limestone cave down there that no one knows about. That is where I work."

"Work? You still work, Uncle Miko," I asked.

"Yes, when I met my demise, I was working to break the *code*, their *code*."

"What *code* are you talking about and who are *they*?"

We walked toward the creek bank. I looked at Uncle Miko and frowned but did not say anything.

"Wait until we get inside and I'll show you."

Uncle Miko pushed aside some low-hanging vines for me to duck under. I could hear the trickling of the water passing over some well-placed rocks, shunting the stream away from a mysterious section of the creek bank. The section rose above the slowly sloping bank and jutted out slightly. It appeared that no one had been there for years. An old alligator slid without a sound into the clear water of the creek. I shivered. Mosquitoes buzzed around me but did not bite because I had been inoculated. Uncle Miko swatted them with the dingy bill of his cap. Uncle Miko held back the scuppernong vines and I saw the cave entrance.

"Come in, my dear. This is my home."

I was stunned. Inside was a fully functioning home, built back into the creek bank. Oddly, a bank of computers lined one wall. Each one displayed odd and constantly changing data on its screen. The machines seemed to be from a bygone era, but the images on the screen looked much like the ones I had seen in Bjorn's basement.

"Quite nice, isn't it? I started building it long before they came for me that day. I knew they would come. I have enough weapons and ammunition to hold off an army, but I know that would only last so long, so this is my only way of surviving. If I destroyed one army, they would just send another. If they ever found me, I wouldn't even get the pleasure of a trip to Paradise Valley; I'd meet my maker before the train reached the station. They have their ways, and no one would ever know about it because I've been *gone* for quite some time. They knew damned well the train didn't get me, but that was a nice story for them to tell. If news had gotten out that I had escaped, it would have caused all kinds of problems for them. They searched for me for months then hoped I actually had died of my injuries.

They were already mostly in charge by that time, so nothing was said about my disappearance. They managed to get a body to bury, really no problem for them, but the casket was closed because of my *extensive injuries*, so no one ever knew I was still alive except Bjorn, of course. They knew I had some of their equipment and I knew what to do with it, but they never found me or the equipment. I burned the farmhouse to the ground before they got there, but they searched the remains. I had moved my electronics to the cave before I set fire to the building, and no one except me, at that time, knew about the cave."

I must have looked like a fool staring at Uncle Miko. Just then I heard breathing behind me and I froze. "Uncle Miko, I hear someone breathing." I didn't move a muscle until I felt something cold and wet touch my hand. I screamed and jumped into Uncle Miko's arms.

Instantly, he began to laugh. "Turn around, Yona, and meet my friend, Tom." I turned around and was face to face with the largest wolf I have ever seen. He was nearly black and his yellow eyes stared at me. I stood very still, but I could feel him smelling my hand.

"On no, will he bite me?"

"No, I can promise you he will not harm you

in any way, but he will destroy anyone who touches you. He's very old like me, but he's still quite strong, and he is and always has been completely fearless. He's been with me since he was born. His mother brought him to me. She was with me for many years and remained with me long after Tom was born. I don't know what happened to her other cubs, but she brought only Tom to me. Her den was near this cave, but she knew they would both be safe here in my domain. And they have been useful several times. We share our food and our shelter with another friend. Look outside the entrance in the tree beside the creek. See the large nest high up in the tree?"

"Yes." The light was blinding for a moment since I had been inside in the semi-darkness, but I could see a large nest high above the creek.

"That's our sentry's home. An eagle we call Phoenix lives there. She's lived here ever since I came here twenty years ago. She got tangled in some briars not long after I came here, and I was able to release her. Since that day, she has been returning the favor. She flies over Tom when he hunts and alerts him to prey, then she follows him home. We dine together, each of us taking only our fair share. It's quite symbiotic, really. I prefer these friends to some I've met in the more "civilized" world. I hope you understand your world is not a good place to be these days."

When I got my wits about me and settled down enough to allow Tom to sniff and approve me, I asked, "Uncle Miko, Paradise Valley isn't really Paradise, is it?"

"No, my dear, it isn't. I worked for the Bureau when I first got out of college. They kept all of us in separate work areas so no one would know what the other scientists were doing, but a few of us managed to communicate. Eventually we formed a group whose goal was to overthrow the establishment.

I don't actually know what happened, but somehow they found out about us and one by one, our group members started disappearing. I knew they would get me, so I came here and prepared to escape. By then, no one lived outside the city, so no one ever came here. I was very close to breaking their code when they got to me, but they didn't know I had already stolen some of the computers and could run them with power generated by this small stream, so I'm still working on the code. Occasionally I am able to break through, but I don't know if I will live long enough to complete my mission. I'm not the only one who escaped, but I can't tell you any more about the others. Just know that we are still working."

"Uncle Miko, is there any way you can help me to get a dispensation to avoid boarding that dreadful train now?"

"I don't know, Yona. You would be better off to stay with me. If you go back now, they will know you have come out here, and that will not help your case. They will ask you why you came here. Most likely they will drop your case if you say no more, but you will be assigned to a train on your 65th birthday.

You have a choice to make. I can scramble your device and disable your chip so they won't know you are here, but if you go back, they will come for you and want to know why your chip has been disarmed. You will have to go in to have another one inserted. It will not go well for you. You can tell them you misplaced your device and don't know what happened to it, but they won't like that either. You can try to tell them your chip might have been damaged by your fever when you were ill. They may not swallow any of those excuses. You have a decision to make."

"Uncle Miko I have three very special young people whom I work with privately. They have such promise. They might be able to change the world, but if I abandon them now, they cannot. If I could just get two more years with them, it might make a difference. I promised myself the day I graduated from college that I would leave the world a better place. How can I give up now?"

"You must walk your own path, my dear. No one can choose it for you, but pick your way carefully. You might live many more years here with me, but if you go back, they will come for you, one way or another. But is that truly the only reason you want to go back?" Uncle Miko smiled softly at me.

"I suppose you know it isn't."

"Yes, I suspect that there is a man behind your hesitance."

"Yes, there is. I am willing to die to be with him."

"Trust me, you can be with him even if you stay here."

I returned his smile. I could see that he knew everything. I leaned back against the cave wall behind the bench I was sitting on. Time was not on my side, either path I chose. If I stayed with Uncle Miko much longer, I would be missed. If I went back, I would face consequences for my journey to the countryside. The clock was ticking. I heard the stream flowing outside the cave entrance. A bird chirped in the distance. And then there were my students to think of. What would become of them? I have given them just enough knowledge for them to become curious and suspicious. Their lives are in my hands. And Bjorn, what will become of the two of us—either way?

"Uncle Miko, I don't know what to do."

"Nor do I, my dear."

"I think I will walk along the creek for a

while."

"Very well. Mind the big alligator on the other bank. He's got a nasty attitude sometimes. Don't take too long. You will be missed, and they will soon realize I am your Uncle Miko. I'm going to scramble your device and disable your chip so they will not know where you are. I'll erase all records for the last 24 hours, but that will come up on their radar tomorrow morning, so you must decide by then."

I turned back toward him. He looked strong and much younger than his 85 years. He is still a powerful man. I paused and held onto the cold stone wall when I asked him, "Uncle Miko, my friend Lillian…do you remember her? She was my good friend when we were kids."

"Yes, I remember her. Why?"

"She turned 65 on the Ides of March. She got on the train. She messaged me when she got there. I think I know what happened to her. Will you tell me what happens when we get to Paradise Valley?

"Yona, I'd rather not."

"I need to know."

Uncle Miko walked toward me and put his still powerful arms around me. He hugged me close and spoke very softly with his mouth near my ear, "Yona, you know what happened. Let it go. You can't help Lillian now. I'm sorry. I know you have talked to Bjorn. I know what Lillian wrote to you. You are correct in your assumption. Just let it go. I will destroy Paradise Valley, but I could not do it in time to help Lillian. The only way I can assure your safety is for you to stay with me. Will you consider doing that?"

My knees nearly gave way, but I knew I could not stay. Uncle Miko looked at me and knew. He leaned down and kissed me on the forehead. I smiled at him and walked away. I didn't look back because I didn't want him to see my face. He nodded and held my hand for one long moment when I turned away. Then he dropped my hand and pushed back the vines for me.

I heard his steps behind me. He walked to the entrance to the cave and watched me go. After walking a ways down the creek bank, I picked a leaf from a camphor tree, crushed it between my fingers and held it to my nose. I inhaled the medicinal scent of the leaf then dropped it to the ground. I walked slowly and steadily up the hill toward the barn. By the time I reached the barn, the rusty lock had been removed and the door stood open.

The drive home was lonely and unsettling, but I knew I had to return. I would rather die with Bjorn than to live without him, and I felt some obligation to Natasha and to other students I had yet to teach. My world is definitely no Utopia, but I need to remain there at least for the present. I have unfinished business and I have finally found a reason to live. Strange how strong the survival impulse can be when we cease to care about our own safety.

Emotions stabbed at me from all directions. I have never been so terrified and so bold at the same time. Let them kill me, but I will not get on that train. I know they will kill me, but it no longer matters. I will not be the one who "on honey-dew hath fed, and drunk the milk of Paradise." There is no Paradise either here or there.

9
A SAVAGE PLACE

Yona returned home conflicted about the future but determined to do whatever it took to stay with Bjorn. She was not afraid for herself, but she realized she had no control over her future. When she unlocked her door, she heard movement inside the room. She opened the door a bit more and peered inside. The door led directly into her small kitchen. She looked around the room. Her eyes came to rest on the small round table. She saw a bit of a very white hand holding onto the floor as if she thought she might fall. She recognized the hand.

She closed the door as quietly as possible and bent down to look into Natasha's tear-streaked face. She put her hand to her lips and motioned for the girl to follow her toward the basement. The girl knew exactly what to do. She crawled out of sight of any windows toward the basement door. When Yona opened the door, both women went inside and Yona quietly closed the door then bolted it from inside.

Yona put her arms around Natasha and said, "Oh, baby girl, what's wrong?"

"Yona, they took him, he's gone! I'm so scared!" The tears flowed like rivers now.

"Who, Natty, who did they take?" Yona knew in her heart, but she didn't want to know.

"Bjorn, they took Bjorn!"

"Who took him?

"Loki's Nine! They took him. I saw it all from the peep-hole in the door. Oh, Yona, what can we do? They will kill him, you know they will! Help me, please!" The girl pleaded.

"Natasha, you are going to have to do something for me before I can go to help Bjorn."

"Anything! Anything! Just tell me and I'll do it!"

Yona pulled an ancient metal box from a drawer and opened it. The hinges were rusty and one broke as she opened the box but the contents were safe. She took out a very sharp knife with a small slanted blade, then she took off her shirt.

"Natasha, I need you to remove the chip in my back. Cut it out."

"Oh Yona, I can't do that," the girl cried.

"Yes, you can. If you don't, I have no

chance whatsoever to save Bjorn. Do it! Now!" Yona said as she handed the scalpel to Natasha.

She handed an alcohol swab and said, "Now, can you feel the chip?"

Natasha rubbed her fingers over the area where all the chips were implanted then she said, "Yes, it's right here. But Yona, this will hurt. I can't hurt you!"

"It won't hurt, I promise you, it won't. What will hurt me is not getting to Bjorn in time. Go, girl, get it done!"

Natasha wiped the skin with the alcohol wipe then took out another one and cleaned the blade. She winced as she made a small cut and blood began to ooze out. She pressed the area beside the chip and saw one edge of it emerge.

"When you see the chip, take these tweezers and pluck it out just like you would a splinter. Come on now, get it done!" Yona had not winced or moved a muscle when Natasha made the cut.

Natasha did as she was told and pulled the bloody chip out. She laid it on the used alcohol wipe and took a bandage from the box. She wiped the blood from the blade and laid it carefully back in the box beside the box of bandages. She pasted the bandage in place, and Yona quickly picked up her shirt and put it back on. She wrapped the chip in a sheet of paper and stuffed it into her pocket.

"Natasha, where is your chip? I'm guessing

you don't have one because if you did, Loki's men would have found you."

Natasha smiled and said, "Oh my chip is in Amsterdam with my sister. She takes it with her every time she goes to the university. They are quite satisfied that I am earning a degree there. Since my father is a physician, he removed my chip before he left and took it with him. I don't intend to ever have a chip again. I don't want to be tracked or controlled. As soon as I am able, I will leave Ragnarock and join my family."

Yona's backbone straightened. She stood up and reached for the cabinet beside the blue chair. "Well, my dear, that might be sooner than you think. I seriously doubt you will ever return to those gates. As soon as I see you safely inside the cave with Miko, I will go back for Bjorn. Miko will see that you get to safety." She pulled out a Glock 9mm and a deer rifle with a powerful scope mounted on it. It was accurate to 300 yards. She gathered two boxes of ammo then led the girl back up the stairs and stepped outside the back door where she kept her car.

Yona stood quietly on the back porch and listened although she no longer cared if she was seen. The worst had already happened or maybe not. She still had hope, but she had to get Natasha to safety first, then she would go for Bjorn, if he was still alive. She envisioned herself bursting into the room shooting everyone in sight. Rage and fear blinded her to the absurdity of that thought.

As Yona stood on her back porch, she heard a rustling in the tree beside the driveway. She looked up and saw a large eagle spreading his wings. She knew that had to be Phoenix. She opened the paper wrapping around the chip and laid in on the porch railing. The eagle gracefully left the tree limb and lit on the railing beside her. The bird picked up the chip with his sharp talons and flapped his powerful wings then was gone. The two women watched as he soared in the afternoon sky and flew off to the South.

The women walked silently to the waiting car. Yona got into the driver's seat and told Natasha to get in the back seat and lie down. The girl did as she was told. Yona tucked the rifle under the blanket in the back floorboard and laid the pistol on the seat next to her.

The car began to move and Natasha asked, "Yona, why did that eagle take your chip?"

"It still had blood and flesh on it. The bird thought it was food."

"But you smiled at the bird and called her Phoenix."

"It's a long story. You will understand later. Uncle Miko will explain. We'll see the bird again. I'm quite sure of that. The eagle's name is Phoenix." Natasha looked at the side mirror on the car and saw the bird flying south as they sped toward the north. Once they were outside the gates, they saw almost no traffic.

Yona rushed headlong into what she hoped would be a rescue mission to save Bjorn. Natasha remained hidden as Yona drove mostly in silence, but as they left the city lights, the girl said quietly, "We can't save him can we?"

"Oh yes we can! I will not let Loki have him. He can have me but not Bjorn. I'll kill him with my last breath!"

"But Yona, how will you know where he is?"

"I know. We have our ways."

Natasha sat up when they were out in the dark countryside. She said, "You are in love with him, aren't you?" It was the first time Natasha had smiled since they took Bjorn away.

Yona glanced in the rearview mirror and appreciated the smile. She returned the smile and replied, "I'm afraid so, dear. Does that surprise you?"

"Yes, I suppose it does. I guess I never thought about his having a girlfriend. I don't remember his ever seeing anyone before. He's always been so serious about his work. That seemed to be who he is…just a scientist. I didn't mean that in a bad way. I just didn't think of him as a man…oh no that's still not what I mean. But I'm glad you love him. I think he is in love with you too. Anytime I mention you, he gets a certain look on his face. Oh Yona, I'm so afraid. What will I do if you can't get to him?"

"I will!"

They drove on in silence, the car picking up speed as they got further away from the compound of Ragnarock proper. The commune owned a vast number of acres but the citizens rarely left the gates. Yona saw the lane ahead and slowed almost to a stop.

"You can sit up now, Natasha. No one will see us from here on in."

"We are going to the cave, aren't we?"

"Yes, have you been there before?"

"No but Bjorn has told me a lot about it. He loves your Uncle Miko like a father. His father died when he was very young and his mother died right after he started college so Miko has been his closest companion all the years since. You know they were together when Miko was supposedly killed. My father tried to be a father to him but Bjorn always wanted to go his own way. He's a truly amazing man."

Yona smiled, "Yes, you don't even know how amazing he is. There, see that barn? We will leave the car in there for a few minutes while I get you to Miko. You will be safe there."

Miko saw their lights approaching and ran

toward the barn. He knew it was bad if Yona came in the night when he had told her not to come back. He got to the barn just as they did. He unlocked it and motioned with his flashlight for her to drive in.

When they were safely inside, Yona and Natasha got out. Yona ran to her uncle and threw her arms around him. "I have to go back. Please take care of Natasha. Loki has Bjorn. I have to go. I will kill Loki. He will most likely kill me, but I will make him release Bjorn."

Miko held her away from him and looked her squarely in the eyes. "No you will not go. You will stay here with Natasha. I will go. They will not kill him right away. It's me they want. I'm old. It's a fair trade. You and Bjorn can carry on my work."

Miko noticed the gun on the seat and grabbed it then found the rifle in the back seat. "And what did you intend to do with these?" he asked.

"Kill Loki!"

Miko laughed and said, "Come with me." Miko led the way down to the creek, carrying the guns.

"No, I have to go. You don't understand!" Yona argued.

"You really think I don't ?" He laughed. "Have you forgotten that I can read your thoughts?"

"Well then you should know why I have to go. I will!"

"No, my dear, you will not. If you go, you will both be killed. Now that wouldn't do me much good, would it? Then I'd just be a lonely old man. We can't have that. Bjorn and I have a plan and this is part of it. It is just a bit sooner than we had planned. Don't worry. The time is right. It is me they want and I will bring down the wrath of the Gods on Loki and his Nine. Loki will be no more and Paradise Valley has claimed its last innocent victim."

They reached the entrance to the cave. There was a lantern burning and a book lying on a stone beside a chair. Miko laid the loaded weapons beside the book. He stepped back to the entrance to the cave and put two fingers between his lips. He made a shrill wavering noise, and they heard something crashing through the bushes at full speed. Tom appeared almost instantly.

"Tom, take care of the girls. Whatever they do, do not let them leave the cave. Guard them with your life."

"Girls," he said with total authority, "Sit down and make yourselves comfortable. Yona give me the code to your car. Tom will destroy anyone who comes near you, and Phoenix will be back soon. He will circle the area to keep you safe. I will send Bjorn as soon as I can, but I may be delayed a while. Shoot anyone else who comes near but please don't shoot Bjorn." He grinned broadly and strode out the entrance, disappearing into the night. He looked every bit like a knight going into battle, but he had no shield and no sword, or at least none were visible.

Yona and Natasha stared at each other with wide eyes. Then Natasha looked at the large almost black wolf standing at the entrance to the cave. Finally Natasha whispered, "Dr. Maheegan, do you think he will hurt us?"

Yona laughed. "Natasha, I promise you, he will not hurt you. I would not try to pet him if I were you, but he's not going to bite you. He will most likely try to push you back into the cave if you try to leave. We are most definitely his prisoners for the present time. We can make ourselves at home."

"Do you think your uncle can save Bjorn?"

"I don't know, but if anyone can, he can. I can't hear Bjorn thinking right now, so I am afraid he is too late. Most of the time, if I try very hard, I can hear him or at least feel his presence. I can feel Uncle Miko thinking, and I think I know what he is trying to do. I sense his thoughts. I am sure my little car is being pushed to its max speed right now. It is very old, but it still moves pretty well."

Miko sped along at well over 100 mph and although his engine made no noise, the tires sang a shrill song of impending disaster. The pavement seemed to blur with the tires. Trees became sparser as he approached Ragrarock. Soon he could see the gates. The gates were open so he flew through them. Sirens went off as he did. His speed set them off. The sirens were still wailing as he flew down the central avenue straight up to the steps of the administrative building. Loki's men were waiting with assault weapons trained on the car. They surrounded him when he stopped. He opened door and one of the guards shoved a gun in his chest.

"Get out of my way, you imbecile! It's me Loki wants, so he's got me! Now take me to him…NOW…you fool NOW!!!"

The guards exchanged looks and one motioned for them to take Miko inside. He was surrounded by automatic weapons as he mounted the steps. The glass doors were thrust open and the group walked in as one. The party moved to the elevator and went directly to the top floor.

Miko was enraged. He could not hear Bjorn's thoughts, so he thought he was too late. But when they arrived at the top floor, he could see why he could not hear Bjorn. The entire floor was fortified with concrete and steel. Nothing penetrated those barriers, nothing. Loki had called for the construction of his personal quarters as a bastion of protection. One of the guards spoke to the device on his wrist and the door slid open without a sound. They walked into a reception area where three more guards stood at attention. They pressed a button and the inner door slid open, exposing Loki's interrogation room.

Bjorn was strapped into a chair that was conspicuously wired for electricity. His arms were strapped to the arms of the chairs and belts girded his chest. Another strap anchored his head to the back of the chair.

"Turn him loose, you bastard! It's me you want, so let him go. I'm here!"

Bjorn glared at Miko, "No, I'm not going anywhere!"

"Yes, hell, you are. You are leaving here. I'm staying."

Loki laughed his sinister laugh, "Yes, you are both staying right here. Your young man is smarter than I thought," Loki said. You will both die right here in front of me, and I will have the joy of watching you both suffer a long and painful demise."

"I'm sure you would enjoy that, but if you do, your world will cease to exist. Watch that window. Precisely at midnight, you will see smoke rising above your precious Paradise Valley for the last time. You will see bits of Paradise fly into the night sky as they explode. I have set explosives to detonate when the clock strikes 12:00. That will be quite a fireworks show. You like fireworks, don't you Commissar?" Miko said. He mocked the Commissar's sinister laugh and spat into his face.

"You arrogant bastard, you don't even know

where Paradise Valley is. You think I don't know the game you are playing." Loki had begun to sweat and Miko knew he had him trapped.

"How about we place bets on that? You want the coordinates of its exact location? Oh, I forgot, you aren't intelligent enough to understand such things as that. I assure you I know where it is. I assume you know where the little bell hangs beside the lamp made of alabaster, the one precisely thirteen steps from the door to the tower in the center, the one where the cute little gadgets are that release the gasses into each dining room…well, I know where that bell is.

You know the intricately carved antique teak cabinet that the lamp sits on? Well, if you want me to turn the explosives off, all you have to do is release Bjorn. Let him drive away in the car I drove here. When I see him freely exit the gates, I will go with you to Paradise Valley and turn my little switch off.

I will empty the cabinet then you can shoot me or whatever you choose to do, but Bjorn is to go free. Neither you nor your men will ever harm him. It's your choice. You can kill us both right now if you choose to. You have the power, but I don't think you will like what happens next. You don't have the code to reset the explosives even if you get there in time. It will blow up no matter what you do. You touch one wire to reset it and it will blow. The explosion will be such that it will trigger tremors felt for miles and the concussion will bring military jets from Washington. Your little experiment will come to light for the entire nation. What do you think will happen then?" Miko's laugh echoed off the iron clad walls. "Remember Waco!"

Loki swore and sat staring at Miko for a long moment. "Let the young bastard go!" he told the guards. It was 10:45. He still had time to get to Paradise Valley before midnight.

The guards started unstrapping Bjorn. As they peeled off the leather restraints, Miko could see burns where they had shocked him. Bjorn rubbed his wrists and shook his head so that his hair fell down over the burn marks. Now Miko could read his thoughts and he could read Miko's. Bjorn nodded to Miko as the guards ushered him out. They exchanged smiles that left Loki more uneasy. It was all going exactly as they had planned.

"I will watch him go. I will not leave this room until I see his headlights outside the gates." According to pre-arranged signals, Bjorn knew to flash the lights twice when he was safely outside and no one was following. If anyone appeared to be following him, he would flash once but if not, he would flash twice. If they flashed only once, Loki would have to shoot Miko because he would not leave the room alive.

"Don't you move an inch! Sit right where

you are. I'll tell you when he's out the gate."

"You can shoot me right now, or you can let me walk to the window. Your choice. But I don't leave this room unless I watch him exit the gates."

Loki swore under his breath, but he did not try to stop Miko. Miko strode leisurely to the window and saw Bjorn start the car. Bjorn already knew the code to Yona's car. The car drove slowly away. He drove toward the gate at barely 20 mph with Loki swearing as he watched. "Get the hell out of here, you imbecile."

"Seems to me you are the imbecile. You've been had. He knows you can't stop him or you lose everything. Never thought that would happen, did you?"

Loki drew back to hit Miko. "I wouldn't do that if I were you. You might injure my pinkie, and I need it to stop the explosion, remember?"

Loki's face was crimson with rage, but he did not move a muscle. "There! He's outside the gates! Go!"

"No, I didn't get the signal yet. Just wait."

Loki looked at his watch. It was 11:15. At best, Paradise Valley was a 40 minute drive.

Miko smiled and said, "Ok, we can go now." He saw Bjorn flash the lights twice and floor the accelerator of the little old car. It sped away fishtailing for the first few seconds. New cars could not do that, but he knew Bjorn would get to the girls before the explosion.

The guards rushed Miko down to Loki's private car. They shoved him inside and Loki got into the front seat beside his driver, who was dressed smartly in black leather. Another guard got into the back seat beside Miko. The heavily armored sedan was not capable of the speeds Yona's small car could make so they didn't arrive at Paradise Valley until 11: 52.

Bjorn arrived at the cave at 11:40. Miko smiled when he sensed Bjorn's thoughts as he saw the girls. Tom trotted along beside them as they ran to Bjorn. Bjorn scooped them up, one in each arm. Both of the women were sobbing, and Tom was circling the three of them. Phoenix had returned and was soaring above them squawking loudly.

Yona recovered her faculties enough to ask, "Bjorn, where is Uncle Miko? Loki has him. doesn't he?"

"Yes, they are on the way to Paradise Valley now. Miko has set explosives to blow it up. Loki thinks Miko will diffuse the explosives. That's why he allowed me to leave."

Yona looked at Bjorn and asked, "He's not going to diffuse them, is he?"

"I think you know the answer to that question."

"I do." She walked away toward the creek then stopped. "Let's go, Bjorn. I want to be there."

"Yes, we are going to be there. Get in the car. I know where Paradise Vallely is. It's not far from here. We can be there by the time it blows. It's not actually set with a timer as Miko told Loki. Miko has to detonate it himself. That was the only way we could get the results we wanted."

"What do you mean?" Natasha asked.

"We need Loki to be destroyed, but even more importantly, such a catastrophic event will bring down the entire world on Ragnarock and show them exactly what is going on inside those sacred walls. If we don't destroy Loki, he will find a way to come back into power. His kind must be eliminated. It is the only way."

Yona closed her eyes and breathed deeply. She understood. They all got in Yona's car and pulled back out onto the main road. They were not far behind Loki's car, so Bjorn drove without headlights. The moon was full and his vision was excellent. He saw the car ahead of him. When he saw Loki's car stop and saw the men getting out, he turned the headlights back on. The men were at the door when they saw him coming. They rushed inside, shoving Miko as they went. Bjorn pulled the car to a stop a quarter of a mile from the gates. He knew what was about to happen.

Miko and Loki followed by the two guards rushed up the stairs to the room with the bell and the alabaster lamp. They were exactly as Miko had described them. Miko opened the cabinet door of the carved teak cabinet and laughed when he saw Loki's face. Loki shouted, "Turn it off, NOW!"

"Sure, Loki," said Miko very calmly then he pressed the red button on the on the inside of the cabinet.

Bjorn, Yona, and Natasha instinctively ducked and covered their heads when the explosion shattered the moonlit night. Bjorn handed Natasha a camera and said, "Go to it, Natty! It's time to see what you learned in Dr. Maheegan's journalism class. Do your stuff, girl. The New York Times is waiting to hear from you. This is your day. Thor just brought the Hammer down!"

Natasha was clicking away before the supplemental explosions had ceased their poundings.

Thirty minutes later, all that was left was a pile of smoking ruins. The full moon gave them a special eerie quality. Some of Natasha's photos would reflect that particular feeling. The smell of the smoke over Paradise Valley would linger for days as proof of what once was. Perhaps it would be a warning for the future, but man is a simple being—he often refuses to see danger written on walls of human construction.

Bjorn and Yona stood beside her car holding each other. Neither one spoke. Yona's face was streaked with tears, but she understood.

Bjorn pointed to a small robot beside the road. He said, "I see someone I know. I'll be right back." Yona looked at him as if he were crazy.

He walked over to the small mechanical servant and picked him up. "Ladies, meet Nostradamus. He knows secrets that will make mankind's head spin."

Natasha walked over to him and asked, "What is that?"

"Well, my dear. This little fellow looks exactly like the other robotic servants conducting business at Paradise Valley, but he belongs to us. He was programmed to meet us here tonight" Bjorn flipped a small tab in the robot's forehead and removed a tiny device. "This small chip contains photos of exactly what happened to the last unfortunate citizens who entered Paradise Valley just last week. You will find undisputable footage of their entry into the dining room, their final conversations, and their reactions as the gas began to exude from the nozzles in the walls and ceilings. You will hear their screams and cries as they tried to escape. Then you will see the automatic scoops come for them and take them to the incinerators. When the bodies have become ashes, you will see those same scoops pick up the ashes and bury them in the pit 50 yards from the building. I'm sure you will be able to sell your article anywhere you like, my dear. Use your skills."

The stillness of the night was broken by the sound of tires whining along the road. Another car was coming toward them. The women stood behind Bjorn as he held his arms out by his side to protect them, then he realized it was Natasha's family. Natalie and her parents screeched to a stop and jumped out of the car. They had been fifty miles away at midnight but even they heard the explosions and felt the earth shake. Bjorn had told them where to meet him, but he delayed them enough to be certain it was over before they arrived.

"What the hell just happened," asked Natasha's father. Her mother was hugging her girls as close to her as she could get them.

Bjorn put his arm around his brother and said, "Well, that's an interesting story."

His brother smiled and said, "I'm sure it is. Miko is gone, isn't he?"

"Yes, he is but he died a happy man, just as he wanted to die. We are all free now because of The Wolf."

"What do you mean? A wolf helped him?"

"No I mean The Wolf killed Loki and set us free."

"I don't understand."

"You will. Maheegan is the Algonquin term for wolf. That's where the name came from. Yona is a wolf also. Now she carries the family legacy. Miko is the term for Chief. Miko was the Chief

Wolf for many years. He was destined to save us. That was his mission—his raison d'être. He fulfilled his destiny beautifully as the old Shaman told him he would. Loki is gone, but his story will live forever as a warning to all."

"How did you know about our heritage, Bjorn?" asked Yona.

"Oh, Miko told me years ago. I could sense his plans from the beginning. None of this was accidental. He had to get Loki into the Paradise Valley compound at midnight. You don't think Loki could have caught me on his own, do you? Our plan had been evolving for more than a year."

"Why didn't you tell me?"

"We were afraid you would try to get involved—after all, you are a wolf also. We knew too much information could be dangerous for you. It was you we were trying to save."

"You are probably correct. I'm not sure I could have helped myself. Well, you could have warned me and not scared me to death."

"Oh, I've been trying very hard not to let you hear my thoughts. I guess it worked. You know we can turn that ability off." He laughed and hugged her close to him. The smoldering ruins of Paradise Valley gave the early morning a glow that lasted for days.

Bjorn spoke to his brother softly, "I need to take Yona back to Miko's cave for a while. We need some recovery time. I have some things I need to tell her. Why don't you all drive up to Birmingham and spend the night, and I will call you tomorrow. Yona has had all the excitement she needs for tonight—maybe we all have. Natasha, I'll give you the whole story tomorrow and you can write it up for the Times. I'm sure they will find it quite interesting." With that Bjorn took Yona's hand and led her to the car.

As they drove away, they were met by flashing emergency lights and sirens rising in the night. They pulled to the side of the road and let the caravan pass. The morning would see troops from the Alabama National Guard flooding in to restore order in the chaos of Ragnarock.

Toward dawn smoke still drifted across the horizon. From the edge of the night came the mournful howl of a lone wolf calling to his pack. Only an echo answered him. The sun rose blood red and the howling ceased. Overhead, a large lone eagle soared.

10
THE MILK OF PARADISE

Bjorn and Yona turned onto the lane leading to the Maheegan family farm, or at least where it had once been. The pear and pecan trees were still standing tall as was the chimney of the old farm. Fragrant wisteria vines climbed the remains. They drove on toward the creek and arrived at the barn. Bjorn flung the door wide open and parked the car. Tom wagged his tail as he greeted them. He sniffed the car, looking for Miko.

Bjorn rubbed the wolf behind the ears and said, "Old man, your friend is not coming back. He's waiting for you in the hills. He will always be there as will you. Stay with us until your time comes to join him, and I will take you there."

They walked slowly down to the cave entrance. When they were inside, Bjorn said,

"Yona, sit down. I have something to tell you. It is about Miko. He wanted you to know after he was gone, but not before." Yona sat down on the rock beside the flowing water. Bjorn took a bottle of wine from the crevice in the wall and poured a glass for both of them. He handed one to Yona. Then he began.

"Yona, you are a Maheegan, but the man who raised you was not your biological father. Miko was not your uncle. He was your father," Bjorn said quietly.

Yona stared wide-eyed at him but she didn't speak.

Bjorn continued, "Your mother loved him very much, but she also loved his brother, the man you knew as your father. When Miko was 20 years old, he had a brief affair with your mother. That is how you came to be. Neither Miko nor his brother knew for many years that Miko was your father. The man you knew as your father never knew. Your parents found out later in life that your father was unable to have children. That's why they adopted Quinn. Your father felt very grateful to have you, so he never questioned your parentage. Your mother told Miko not long before she died. She still loved both of them, but she wanted Miko to know. She knew that their lives might be in danger, so she wanted to know that Miko would watch over you. He owed a debt so tonight, he paid that debt. He avenged the deaths of his brother, sister-in-law, nephew and so many others whom he loved. He even felt he was doing this for Lillian."

Yona did not seem surprised. She smiled. "I think I always knew, and I think he always knew too. He loved me too much to be an uncle, and I loved him the same way. I suppose tonight was fitting. I wonder if my parents saw the explosion."

"I'm sure they did. And tomorrow the world will see it also. Natasha will ensure that. She, too, has a story to tell, and because of Miko, she can now tell it."

"Bjorn, could we rebuild the farm and call it Wolf Creek?"

"I'm sure we can. What about opening it as a wolf preserve where we rescue wolves and give them a safe place to live?"

"That sounds appropriate to me, especially since you rescued me."

Phoenix perched in the tree outside the cave and Tom came inside and sat down beside them.

They slept soundly and when they awoke, they heard many heavy vehicles on the main road. They dressed and started for town. They were stopped at the gate outside Ragnarock proper. The guardsman who stopped them asked, "Sir, I'm sorry but we cannot allow you to go inside the gates. Do you have proper ID?"

"Yes, sir. I do. I live in the town and so does the lady. We both own houses there. We need to go collect our things."

After checking their identification, the guardsman said, "Proceed with caution, sir. There is chaos in the town. Their government was destroyed last night and there is massive civil disorder. Just use caution and stay in your homes as much as possible. Our people are working to restore order as quickly as possible. This town was an experiment from the beginning, and it definitely did not end well. There will be guardsmen on every street so don't hesitate to call for help if you need it."

"Thank you, sir. We will use caution." Bjorn looked at Yona and smiled. "Looks like we did our job."

"Yes, but it will be difficult for a while."

"I'm sure it will, but well worth it. Miko gave his life to save us, so it is our job to make the best of what he gave us. We'll stop at my house first and pick up a few things then we can go to your house." As they drove into town, they saw dazed people wandering about. Everyone seemed lost. Finally they arrived at Bjorn's home. They pulled into the driveway and stopped. When they got out, three neighbors came out to greet them.

"Do you know what happened last night?" the first one asked.

"No, what happened?"

"Someone blew up Paradise Valley. Where will we go now? No one knows what do to. I was supposed to go next year. What will I do? I don't have any money. I'll have to find a job just to eat. They took away all our privileges. How will we survive? Where will I find a job? Who is going to take care of us? All the robots have been disabled. Loki kept everything going. Where is he? Why did he abandon us?" the obviously distraught man walked away with the other two following him.

Bjorn didn't bother to answer him. He knew there was no point. It would take years to re-train the people of Ragnarock to exist on their own. They were sheep and now they had no one to shelter and feed them. They were prey for more than 30 years. Man cannot overcome that much training in one generation. Education had all but gone away and motivation had been stifled. The sheep had become mechanical, lazy, and unmotivated. That could not be changed. Anger and resentment was written on the faces of some residents walking in the streets while others merely looked dazed and confused.

They heard gunfire not far down the street and saw men with assault rifles shooting down meandering robots on the sidewalks. The robots had lost their programmers, so they were as dazed as the citizens. The men with guns seemed to be enjoying their new sport.

"Bjorn, I think we should gather our things

and leave as soon as we can. Sooner or later the sheep will figure out that the wolves destroyed the lions and they will want to harm us. We must leave as soon as we can. All I want from my place is my books and my clothes and a few memories. If they see us packing the books, they will stone us. They will know we are guilty. None of them have been allowed books since 2030. They believe them to be dangerous. They will immediately know we had a part in this. That will not go well for us."

"Yes, you are right, Yona. I don't need much either. I need some of the electronics I have, and I need to gather Natasha's things. I don't think she and her family should come back. Let's get this done as soon as we can. We can pack my things in my car then I'll help you pack and we'll go back to Miko's world. That's where we belong anyway."

They packed Bjorn's belongings along with Natasha's, then Yona left in her car, driving toward her house. People were still wandering in the streets. One of her neighbors flagged her down before she could get in her driveway.

"Dr. Maheegan, can you believe what happened? Where is Loki? Do you think the rebels found him? Do you think he will come back? What am I going to do? I worked in Loki's building. Is the building still there or did they destroy it too? Oh, I'm so scared!"

"I'm sorry, Mrs. Marshall. I don't have any

answers. I'm sure we will get some answers soon. It would be better if you would stay inside until all this settles out. You will be ok. I don't think any of the buildings in town were harmed. I was away when it happened. I was visiting relatives. I don't know much right now either, but you should stay inside to be safe. I'm sure you will be ok."

Shortly after that, Bjorn drove up. He pulled his car around to the back where Yona was already gathering her books. She found some boxes and packed them first then loaded the rest into the back seat as quickly as she could. Her clothes and personal belongings, she tossed in quickly on top of the books. When things settled down, she would come back for the blue chair and some of the dishes her mother had used.

All was not lost for her, but most certainly everything had changed. Her world would be new. Suddenly she thought of Lillian and Fred. What would Lillian have thought if she could be here today?

Yona was not sure Lillian would have understood. She was not even sure she understood it all, but she knew life would be better for her. She would try to contact her "special" students and perhaps even teach again, but it would be different. She would never teach again unless she was free.

She stopped for a moment and sat down in the blue chair. "Thank you, Uncle Miko," she said quietly. She allowed a few tears of gratitude to leak from her eyes, then she got up and started her new and final life.

When both cars were packed to the gills, the two vehicles eased out of the driveway, hoping to remain unnoticed. They drove as quickly as was practical to the open gates of Ragnarock and waved to the friendly guard as they left the confines of the sheep and the lions.

Six weeks after the explosion, Yona and Bjorn strode up to the barn and retrieved some tools. They walked toward the crumbling remains of the original farm house. They talked softly as if not to disturb the ghosts lingering in the remains. Bjorn gestured toward the property lines and all four directions. Yona told him there were still 1500 acres in the homestead. Five hundred acres were planted in pine forest that was ready to harvest, but the other thousand acres contained mature pecan, pear, and apple trees plus a vineyard that spanned 10 acres.

"This is the perfect place for our sanctuary," Yona said.

Just as the words escaped her lips, Tom came trotting up to them. He was aging but still majestic and beautiful. He stopped and nudged Bjorn's hand. Bjorn rubbed his head and said, "Welcome home, old boy. We've been missing you.

Where have you been?"

Yona looked out into the pecan orchard and saw a white shaggy shape approaching them cautiously. "I think that's where he's been. I think that might be his lady."

"Well, good for you old boy. Bring your lady to see us."

His lady was snow white. She looked a bit shabby and underfed, but she was home now, so that would certainly change. She was hesitant to approach them. She stood back 50 yards, then Yona made a low howling noise just loud enough for her to hear. The white wolf slowly approached the group as Tom walked out to meet her. He led the way toward Yona, who was speaking to them both in a tongue Bjorn had never heard before.

The white wolf seemed mesmerized by the words. Yona knelt down and the white wolf walked in front of Tom and came very near Yona. Yona moved her head nearer the white wolf, who then rubbed her face against Yona's face. Yona continued to talk to her as she stroked the animal's soft but matted fur.

"See, Bjorn, we are going to create a sanctuary here for Tom's family. His lady will be safe here, and she will never be hungry again. That is what Uncle Miko would have liked. I wonder if this old girl knew him. This is how we honor him. He gave his life to save the good people of

Ragnarock, and now we will devote the rest of our years to saving these magnificent creatures. Tom guarded Natasha and me on a very important night in our lives—now I will guard him for the rest of his.

ABOUT THE AUTHOR

Corinda Pitts Marsh has written stories ranging from a 500 page Civil War novel to smaller biographical non-fiction about growing up in North Florida. With English degrees from the University of Central Florida and Florida State University, she is a retired grandmother who writes to bring change where change is due and understanding where none exists.

PREVIOUS PUBLICATIONS

Holocaust in the Homeland
Behind the Tupelo Tree: Secrets of the South,
    Vols. I and II
A Civil War: Civil Words from Savage Hearts
    Are the Weapons of Small Men
The Ghost of Blackwater Creek
Illusions of Honor: The Truth and the Myth
B'ar Yarns: Florida Pioneer Stories
Shooter Giggers: Diving and Spearfishing in the
    Florida Panhandle in the 1950's
Blue Butterfly Days: Dreams and Regrets
The Magic Dolphin
Eminent Danger
Finding Ann
Satan Wears a Halo
Fins and Friends
Sandspurs and Sunshine

The Smoke over Xanadu